Philip E. Di

A Handbook of
Spiritual Perfection

SOPHIA INSTITUTE PRESS®
Manchester, New Hampshire

Printed in the United States of America.
Cover design: LUCAS Art & Design, Jenison, MI.
in collaboration with Perceptions Design Studios.

Sophia Institute Press
Box 5284, Manchester, NH 03108
1-800-888-9344

www.SophiaInstitute.com
Sophia Institute Press® is a registered trademark of Sophia Institute.

Imprimi potest: Daniel M. Leary, C.M.V., Provincial Superior
Nihil obstat: James F. Rigney, S.T.D., *Censor Librorum*
Imprimatur: Francis Cardinal Spellman, Archbishop of New York

Library of Congress Cataloging-in-Publication Data

Dion, Philip E., 1910-
    A handbook of spiritual perfection / Philip E. Dion.
        p.   cm.
    Includes bibliographical references.
    ISBN 1-928832-40-7 (pbk. : alk. paper)
    1. Spiritual life — Catholic Church. I. Dion, Philip E., 1910- Basic
spiritual means. II. Title.

BX2350.2.D545 2001
248.4'82 — dc21   2001049068

Dedicated to my mother,
Sister Vincent de Paul Dion, R.C.S.,
at whose maternal insistence
this book was written in filial obedience

Editor's note: The biblical quotations in the following pages are taken from the Douay-Rheims edition and the Confraternity edition of the Old and New Testaments. Where applicable, quotations have been cross-referenced with the differing names and enumeration in the Revised Standard Version, using the following symbol: (RSV =).

Contents

Preface

※

This book is intended to instruct you in the precise nature of certain basic spiritual means of sanctification. Unless you know the nature of these means accurately, you cannot use them intelligently, and, moreover, you run the risk of using them badly and consequently being hindered by what is intended to help. Furthermore, unless their nature is understood properly, there is little likelihood of their being used with much enthusiasm or zeal. Experience proves that no small amount of confusion and fuzzy thinking, if not downright ignorance, about the nature of these spiritual means exists among those who sincerely wish to lead holy lives, but fail to achieve results because of faulty or deficient understanding of these matters.

In addition to explaining the nature of the various spiritual means, practical methods are offered for using them profitably and intelligently, not only in themselves, but for integrating them into a unified spiritual life, lived purposefully and determinedly. You will be assisted thereby to contribute maximum glory to God and consequently to reap maximum peace and happiness from your life of service to God.

All that is written in this book is predicated on the fact that many are truly sincere in their desire to seek perfection

A Handbook of Spiritual Perfection

and live a supernatural life. Many failed efforts, of course, are attributable to the weakness of the human will.

But the conviction is inescapable that much more effort is lacking or misdirected because of ignorance than because of weakness, and that many would rise to far greater heights of perfection if they were but aware of the achievability of the heights and were they but challenged to begin to scale them.

That is the purpose of this book!

❧

A Handbook of
Spiritual Perfection

Chapter 1

❧

Motivate yourself
to grow in holiness

❧

Too often a person looks at the past year and beholds only the shambles of the good resolutions he made last year concerning his predominant fault or some virtue he wanted to acquire. Appalled at his lack of success at another year's end, he says once again to himself or to his director, "Why don't I do something about getting that virtue? After all, I want to."

Sometimes, with God's help, the scene a person sees in retrospect is not quite so devastated. But neither is it a picture of magnificent triumph or prodigious progress in virtue. Last year, he had hoped this year would find him quite proficient in the practice of his particular virtue, or considerably more advanced toward victory over his predominant fault or faults. But such is not the case, as it was not the case last year. Yet, both these persons — the complete failure and the doubtfully successful — sincerely believe that they want to have this or that virtue or to overcome their predominant fault.

Why this pitiful progress toward perfection that tends to discourage too many good people? As they so often ask themselves: "Why *don't* I do something practical about getting that virtue or overcoming that fault?" Dismiss immediately as the cause of this failure the lack of God's grace in a soul seeking to advance in perfection. True, without His grace, there can be no progress: "Without me, you can do nothing."[1] But sufficient grace is always present. Failure to advance, then, should be ascribed to a deficiency in personal efforts, which must cooperate with the motions of grace in all supernatural activity, whether it be overcoming faults or practicing virtue.

This being so, deficient efforts and scant progress in overcoming our predominant faults are traceable to the ability every one of us has to deceive ourselves more completely than another could possibly deceive us. We tell ourselves we want this virtue, or we want to get rid of that fault. We think we mean it. But we do not *really* mean it; that is, we do not actually *will* it. If we did, we would be more persistent in seeking and presumably more successful in achieving what we say we want.

True, we admire the virtue speculatively. We think it would be nice to have. But thinking thus, we often subconsciously say to ourselves, "But it is such a lot of trouble to get it. Do I really want it enough to make all that continued effort? After all, we can overdo this seeking for perfection. I will try for a while, but if it gets too difficult, I will drop it." Generally, that is what happens. Or, without going so far as to entertain such cowardly and defeatist thoughts, even subconsciously, we often conclude that because we admire a virtue speculatively, we therefore have a sincere desire for it. Such notions, says St. Vincent de Paul,[2] are "the products of the mind which, having

---

[1] John 15:5.

[2] St. Vincent de Paul (c. 1580-1660), founder of the Lazarist Fathers and the Sisters of Charity.

found some facility and sweetness in the consideration of virtue, flatters itself with the idea that it is actually virtuous." Such speculative admiration or desire for a virtue will not produce the virtue automatically in a soul. Moreover, it will never move the will to adopt means to acquire it by personal effort.

It is only when I conceive a good as practicable and *good for me* that my will is moved to do something about getting that good. Not a speculative judgment, but a *practical* judgment about the goodness of a thing for me, moves my will to action.

Holding a tablespoon out to her little son with a stomachache, a mother says, "Here, take this castor oil. It's good for you." Oh, yes? The little son is not convinced of that thesis. Speculatively, he might admit that it might be good for *some* people or some people's stomachaches. But he has not come to a practical judgment that it is good for him. Nor does he intend to. Thus, only by coercion, and not voluntarily, will he take the castor oil, if indeed he does take it.

But who will coerce me to overcome my predominant fault? Unless I convince myself by a practical judgment that the unpleasantness of fighting my predominant fault, or the distastefulness of effort involved in acquiring a particular virtue, is good for me, is the only course for me, I will *never* tackle the job.

Lack of motivation, then, must be blamed in the first place for scant progress in overcoming a predominant fault or in acquiring some particular virtue. Our progress is negligible because we have not properly motivated ourselves. Our intellect has not made the possession of that virtue or the being rid of that fault appear as a sufficiently *practical, personal good for us.* Yet this is the first step that we must take on the road to improvement. Until we are properly motivated to get rid of a fault or acquire a virtue, we can study, or search for, or have pointed out to us all the *means* in the world, but we shall never *begin to do*. Until we have motivated ourselves to say, "I *want* this, and with the help of God's grace, *nothing* will keep me from it," no amount of instruction or direction as to means will have any result.

You must motivate yourself

In the final analysis, the responsibility for motivation rests squarely on the shoulders of each individual. Only we ourselves can penetrate our own will and motivate it to act. Motives can be pointed out to us, but unless our own intellect assimilates them and presents the goal to our own will as a *desirable good for us,* it will all be "sounding brass and tinkling cymbals."[3] Motivation and determination must come ultimately from within the individual. Until it does, until it is present, little progress will be made in acquiring virtue or overcoming faults.

Since motivation looms so large in the process of overcoming a predominant fault, we should be clear on how to achieve it. How do we motivate ourselves in a practical way, so that our will will spring into action in seeking any particular good?

• *Consider the virtue or vice.* Obviously, before the intellect can present cogent motives to the will, it must itself

---

[3] Cf. 1 Cor. 13:1.

be convinced of the goodness and desirability of the object in question. Such conviction comes only from the operation of the mind on the truth of the matter at hand, since the proper object of the mind is truth.

The intellect, then, must perform its threefold operation of apprehension, judgment, and reasoning on the truth about the particular virtue to be acquired or the particular vice to be uprooted. To express it more plainly, although perhaps more painfully, we must *meditate!* We must meditate on the nature of the vice or virtue and the various motives that would impel us to attack the vice or embrace the virtue. We must mull over, ruminate, and think about all the compelling reasons for and benefits of having the virtue or not having the vice, until the result becomes appealing and beautiful enough to trigger our will into action to get it.

These motives or reasons can be drawn, first, from faith, by examining our Lord's teaching and example on the subject in question; by examining the example of the saints and perhaps even of our companions. Reason can likewise furnish motives, such as the difficult or absurd or undesirable consequences that would follow taking the opposite course. But for a practice aimed at overcoming a predominant fault or acquiring a particularly needed virtue, the realm of faith will provide the most fruitful supernatural motives to move the will to action.

♦ *Think about the love of God.* No human act is ever performed without a motive. But there is a *hierarchy* of motives. The more powerful the motive is, the more energetically we will work to achieve the envisioned goal. But of all the possible motives that can account for our actions, the most powerful of all is the motive of love. Love is God's own motive. He does all things for love.

Therefore, if we are truly serious about overcoming a predominant fault, the most powerful motive we should try to arouse is the love of God. If we will not undertake the battle against a predominant fault or the seeking of a particular virtue for the love of God, then certainly there is no other worthy motive strong enough to sustain us in that persevering struggle.

The motive of the love of God can be aroused only by persistent and conscientious meditation on the goodness and love that God has first shown toward us. Once we begin to come to the realization of the extent of God's love for us, we cannot help wanting to love God in return.

• *Pray.* Then, add to meditation unceasing, earnest prayer to beg God for the grace to love Him enough to want to combat your predominant fault.

Since, then, meditation plays such an important part in the process of supernatural self-motivation, we must have clear ideas about it. Hence, it will be advantageous to interpose at this point a treatment of mental prayer before proceeding in the discussion of the combat with our predominant fault.

Chapter 2

༞

Think about
your Faith

❧

For the most part, we do not naturally have a true appreciation for things of the supernatural. Yet the difference between those who have and those who do not have a real appreciation for the supernatural is the difference between the saints and us. The holier a person is, the greater his appreciation of things supernatural, and, conversely, the greater a person's appreciation and realization of things supernatural, the holier he is, because it is that appreciation, that realization, which moves him to supernatural action. It is not how much we know, but how *well we realize* what we know of the truths of our Faith that influences our living.

Thus, if we are to become any holier, if we are even to become canonizable saints, it will not be because we shall have learned anything new. If we are to grow holier, it will follow only upon greater self-motivation, which, in turn, will come from a greater *realization* of the meaning of the truths of our Faith.

We probably know more now in the way of scientific exposition of the truths of our Faith, more of the strictly theological content of the truths taught by Christ, than perhaps the saints did, than St. Peter did in his day, before there was a development of the science of theology. We know the truths more explicitly, but the saints realized to a much greater degree what they knew than we do. Actually, we *know* many things that we *don't realize*. We rattle off the Apostles' Creed, but we seldom realize the implications of what we are saying.

This fact of unrealized knowledge can be easily demonstrated. Things known have not hit us with the impact needed to make us truly *realize* what it is that we know. For example, we have heard and reacted many times to the term "a billion dollars." Now, we know what a billion dollars is; we know it is a thousand million dollars. That, of course, is a lot of money! But do we realize just how much money it is? Most probably we don't.

Get a picture of it in this way: if we had a million dollars in brand-new thousand-dollar bills, we would have a pile of bills eight inches high. But, if we had a *billion* dollars in brand-new thousand-dollar bills, we would have a pile of bills 155 feet higher than the Washington monument — over 666 feet high! Imagine a pile of thousand-dollar bills over 666 feet high, and you are seeing one billion dollars. Now when we read that the national budget calls for 174 billion dollars' expenditure, we have a faint realization of what that budget is, because we realize what one billion dollars is.

Learn to realize the truths of your Faith

How did we get that realization? We got it by comparing a billion dollars with things that we know. We compared it with inches and feet; we compared it with the Washington monument, with the height of a building fifty stories high. We have pictures of those things already in our mind. Then, when we took the thing that was not known so clearly and compared it with what was known, we started to get a realization from our thinking, comparing, recalling, and so on.

Only in this way shall we begin to get a realization of the truths of our Faith that we enumerate so blithely in the Apostles' Creed. We know, for example, the fact of death. But do we *realize* it? Any one of us standing before a group of people could truthfully say, "I know that you are going to die, and that your sister is going to die, and that you over there are going to die, but I am not going to die." Isn't that the way we all think? We picture everybody else dead but ourselves. Did we ever picture ourselves laid out in our coffin and wonder how we are going to look? That is the way to realize death. It is going to come surely! What is the sense of being an ostrich, putting our head in the sand and pretending that it is not? It was such a picture and a realization of death that turned St. Francis Borgia from a courtier into a saint.[4]

Again, we say that we realize what sin is; at least we say we know that sin, even venial sin, is the greatest evil in the world, the only real evil. Yet, does that knowledge deter us from committing venial sin?

We say we know and believe that Christ is present in the Blessed Sacrament. We say we know that, but do we realize it? It is the same Christ who walked the streets of Galilee and

---

[4] St. Francis Borgia (1510-1572), Duke of Gandia who later became a Jesuit priest.

cured the sick and healed the blind and forgave sinners and raised the dead to life, the same Christ who put His hands on the heads of little children and blessed them. He is there in the tabernacle when we go into the church for a visit or for Mass. We believe that, but do we realize it? If we did, how can we account for our attitude? Can we imagine sitting in His physical presence and having our minds wander? Can we imagine our being able to go in and out of a room where He was physically present without realizing where we had been or what we had done? Can we imagine our being distracted by something else if we realized who was there? Thus, it won't be learning any new truths about His Real Presence in the Blessed Sacrament that will turn us into an adorer and lover of Christ in the Blessed Sacrament. It will only be a *realization* of a truth we already know.

What we need in general are real convictions about the supernatural that will regulate all our actions. But the problem is how to get them. In seeking the answer to this question, we might ask ourselves how we or anyone get convictions in life about anything? How do people get convictions about what they are going to do with their lives, about how they are going to perform some series of actions? How do they get convictions and reach decisions on important affairs in their lives? How do they decide on a vocation — whether they are going to marry, whether they are going to marry this person or that; whether they are going to follow this career or another career; whether they are going to be a doctor, or a lawyer, or a nurse, or a teacher, or whatever? How does anybody get convictions about these things?

In a word, they *think* about the problem; they weigh it with all its pros and its cons: "What will be the advantages if I follow this course of action and the disadvantages if I follow the other course of action? If I follow the other course of action, what will be the advantages? What will be the disadvantages?" So they weigh both propositions until they find which is the most advantageous, and, considering all things, they come to a prudent decision. In other words, they think about the thing; they ponder, they reflect upon it.

Pondering your Faith helps you live in accordance with it

There we find the reason we do not have convictions about the supernatural, about the truths of our Faith, convictions that really affect our lives. It is because we have not pondered, we have not thought about them. We have not weighed them. As the Holy Spirit tells us, "With desolation is the whole world made desolate because there is no one who considereth in his heart."[5]

We have failed to develop a spiritual sanctuary within us. We have not discovered the spiritual powers within us, and by *spiritual* here is meant not the supernatural, but our rational power to think and reflect. We have within us a whole world hidden from all but ourselves. It is the world of spirit in which we share in the likeness of God. It is the realm of thought where we can escape from the prison of our external surroundings and fly out beyond the trammels of our senses to soar

[5] Cf. Jer. 12:11.

freely in the world of our mind up to the very throne of God. It is a whole kingdom within us where the kingdom of God is and where we can live as rational beings, delighting in things of spirit.

But so much are we creatures of habit, acting mechanically, so used are we to having our thinking done for us, that we have neglected to think and to develop our powers of thought. Thus, because we neglect to reflect on the truths of our Faith, we so easily fall into natural ways of living, natural ways of thinking and judging. We judge of things chiefly by their effects on our material welfare and our physical well-being. In other words, it is possible to live practically without thinking; it is possible to live a most superficial kind of animal existence without ever really tapping the resources of our spiritual mind, without ever becoming familiar with the whole thrilling world of spirit within us.

Because we have not developed our spiritual powers in stride with our physical powers, we have failed to realize the privilege that God has bestowed in giving us those very mental powers and faculties and the ability to exercise them on infinite Truth and Goodness and Wisdom Itself. In a word, we do not appreciate our ability to think about God. We don't realize that we haven't even begun to tap our own mental resources.

Consequently, there is often dislike and sometimes even repugnance for mental prayer, one of the most fundamental elements of all spiritual life. So, if we are to preserve our standard of value, if we are to advance in the spiritual life, we must retire into ourselves and pursue mental activity with at least the same effort as we do physical activity. If we are to grow in the likeness of God, we must, in particular, acquire a facility with the power of mental prayer, which is the greatest kind of intellectual activity possible.

Mental prayer nourishes your soul

The effect of mental prayer on life is the same as the effect of food on our body. Should we omit to feed our spirit through mental prayer, it would produce the same effect in our spiritual life as neglecting to eat food would produce in our physical life.

St. Vincent de Paul, that great man of prayer, says, "A Christian who does not pray is a mere animal in the spiritual life." If a man does not use his spiritual powers, he might as well not have them; and if he did not have them, he would be an animal that lacks rationality, intellection, and volition.

Often spiritual writers tell us that daily mental prayer is like a mirror that we hold up to our souls, as it were. It shows us our spiritual reflection with all of its blemishes just as a material mirror would show us the reflections of our face. But there is this great difference: the material mirror can do nothing but show us the hopeless reflection of our face; having shown it, the mirror can do nothing about changing it. On the other hand, the mirror of mental prayer that we hold up to ourselves not only has the power to show us our defects, but can also point out to us the remedies for the defects. It is through mental prayer, for example, that we motivate ourselves and come to a practical judgment about why it is good for us to have such-and-such a virtue, or that we come to a practical judgment about why it is good for us to get rid of such-and-such a fault.

As was said in the previous chapter, only such a practical judgment moves our will. Motivation is not merely a speculative decision that it is good to have such-and-such a virtue, or that it is good not to have such-and-such a fault. It is a practical judgment that it is good for me to have this virtue, or it is good for me not to have this fault. That practical judgment alone will move us to doing something about acquiring a virtue or getting rid of a fault. And it is through mental prayer, through meditation, that we come to that practical judgment.

So, we can understand that mental prayer is not only the mirror in which we see our defects and discover the virtues we lack, but it is also the means whereby we can remedy those defects. By it we can motivate ourselves and determine upon the means to do so.

There are many other analogies that help us to realize the place of mental prayer in our lives. Teachers know about a tool called the *plan book*, in which the teacher must write down explicitly for each day precisely what matter she is going to teach, what objective she hopes to achieve in teaching it, and what devices or projects she will employ to teach the matter in order to reach these objectives. Frequently and unannounced, the supervisor drops in to inspect the plan book and see that it is up to date.

So, our meditation is, as it were, our spiritual plan book for the day. We talk over with God the objectives we hope to accomplish in overcoming vice and acquiring virtue, and the means whereby we are going to do it. It is our preparation for the day's work, preparation for the heat and the burden of the day in the vineyard of the Lord.

Mental prayer uses your imagination and memory

Mental prayer is simply a conversation with God about Him and us. It is called *mental prayer* to distinguish it from vocal prayer, in which we recite formulas and say them with our lips. Mental prayer, on the other hand, stresses the use of the mental faculties, the memory and the imagination and particularly the mind and the will. Now, there is nothing wrong with talking to God with our lips informally during mental prayer, but essentially it is an exercise of the higher faculties of the mind and will be aided by the imagination and the memory.

First, we use our imagination and memory in mental prayer. Sometimes the point of meditation is read out of a book. This is the "starter" of mental prayer. However, a warning is imperative here. In no sense must the time of mental prayer be turned into a time of uninterrupted reading from a spiritual book. Such a practice of continuous reading during mental-prayer time is a flagrant abuse sometimes indulged in by those unwilling to make the continued effort involved in pursuing mental prayer. Not only does this irregularity rob God of the service of prayer we owe Him, but it also deprives the soul of the strength and nourishment it needs, and which can be obtained in no other way than by mental prayer.

Now, to return to our topic, from the points of meditation or the segment of a book we have read as a "starter," we recall with our memory various scenes from the life of our Lord or examples we have seen of the virtue or the vice in action. If we cannot recall from memory, we can invent them with our imagination. For example, if we have read about some scene in the life of our Lord, we can reconstruct it with our imagination; we can picture our Lord there, or our Blessed Mother, or St. Joseph, if it is the childhood of our Lord. Thus, we use the faculties of memory or imagination.

From these pictures or images thus constructed, we then extract with our mind the ideas that are contained therein. We begin to think of and consider the ideas that are brought up by these images. For example, in the meditation at hand, what virtue is being demonstrated by this saint or by our Lord? What virtue is he practicing, or what vice is He telling us to avoid? Or, it may be that the meditation topic is God Himself or one of His attributes — His goodness, His mercy, His justice, His holiness — or some other truth of our Faith. We think about it. We ask, "What is the lesson in this truth for me? What can I learn from it?" And so on. Or, we ask, "Why should I have this virtue or why should I get rid of this vice?" Thus, we have used our imagination and our memory and ultimately our minds to think about God or some particular virtue or vice. But all of this is really only the preparation for true mental prayer.

Mental prayer calls for an act of your will
We have not begun to pray until we have started to use our *will*. The purpose of this reflection with our mind, the purpose

of thinking in meditation is not to have beautiful thoughts, but that our thoughts might move our will to act, that is, might move our will to *make acts*.

But what is meant by *acts of the will?* Here are some examples: to tell God that we love Him; to tell God that we are sorry for having hurt Him; to tell God we want to make reparation; to tell God how wonderful He is; to tell God we hope in Him or that we believe in Him; to tell God that we would like to console Him for all the sins that were committed last night — all these are acts of the will. It is only when we begin to make such acts as these with our will that we begin to get at the heart of prayer, that we really pray.

There is nothing wrong, as has been said, with vocalizing these acts with our lips, telling God in our own words that we love Him. There is nothing wrong with such speaking, but it is not necessary. We can tell Him all that with just a glance of the heart looking up at the tabernacle. We can tell God that we love Him, or that we are sorry, or that we hope in Him, or how wonderful He is, or how much we thank Him, or we can ask Him for something, all without a word passing our lips.

These acts of the will are sometimes called *affections* in spiritual books. Because they are called *affections*, many think that they have to be accompanied by a facsimile of goose pimples, which is not true at all. We don't have to *feel* these affections. They are acts of our will, not feelings. Even though we feel cold as ice and dry as ashes, if we kneel in meditation and tell God we love Him, tell Him we're sorry, tell Him we hope in Him, or make any one of these acts as the Holy Spirit moves us to make them, we are praying! That is what we achieve by our affections, and that is the goal we hope to reach by reason of the considerations we have previously thought.

When we have thought in our minds of how wonderful God is, of how good He is, of how good the saints have been, and so on, we are moved to ask Him to make us good, to tell Him we love Him, to tell Him we are sorry. Our will is moved to action by the grace of the Holy Spirit. Just as soon as we feel our will being moved by the Holy Spirit, we should begin to make these acts and continue to make them for as long as we can. If we find that we stop after a while, we can go back to thinking a bit more, like a youngster giving his scooter another push with his foot as he slows down.

But we must keep in mind that we are aiming to make acts of our will. Remember that! Remember, too, that they can be made wordlessly, with a simple glance of the heart, or, if we prefer, we can pronounce them with our lips. God loves them either way.

☙

Mental prayer ends with a resolution

Finally, at the end of our meditation, if it is to be practical, our will will formulate some kind of resolution. But this resolution need not flow directly from or be about the subject of our meditation. First and foremost, it should concern our spiritual practice[6] or predominant fault.

---

[6] The spiritual practice is the particular virtue we are trying to acquire or the particular vice or fault we are trying to overcome. The notion of a spiritual practice and our predominant fault will be treated more fully in Chapter 5.

It is simple to make a resolution that bears on our predominant fault flow from meditation on any subject. Sensibly, we should take the same resolution about that virtue or that vice every day in the week, for weeks or months at a time. We didn't get the bad habit overnight, and we are not going to get the opposite good habit overnight. If we wanted to play the piano, we would not practice the piano on Monday, the drums on Tuesday, the saxophone on Wednesday, the tuba on Thursday, something else on Friday, and on Saturday get back to the piano again, and then repeat the cycle weekly. No, we would practice the piano *every* day of the week. So, too, if we are trying to acquire humility, or simplicity, or charity, or patience, we practice that virtue in particular every day, and that is what we should take a resolution about every day.

But, how can this be done in conjunction with our daily meditation, the subject of which varies each day?

Well, in any meditation, if it has become true prayer in our will, we have been making acts of love of God; we have been telling God with our will that we love Him. Nearing the end of the meditation, the time comes to take our resolution. No matter what the subject of meditation has been, if it has led us to make acts, we are telling God we love Him. It is the simplest thing, then, to say, "And to prove that I love You, dear Lord, I resolve that today at such-and-such a time, in such-and-such a place, I am going to do such-and-such about my particular practice." This can be done whether our practice has anything to do with the topic of meditation or not. The proof of the love we say we have for God is what we do to show our love.

A Handbook of Spiritual Perfection

In this way, we can make a resolution about our practice flow from any meditation. For example, again, suppose we are making acts of reparation to God. At resolution time, we can say, "And to show You that I want to make reparation, I resolve today that at such-and-such a time, in such-and-such a place, when I am tempted to do such-and-such, I am going to do thus-and-so as an act of reparation."

Again, suppose we were making acts of sorrow: "To show You that I am sorry for having offended You in the past, I am going to do such-and-such today." That is, I renew my resolution about my particular practice. But it is substantially the *same* resolution each day.

Now, of course, there is no law against taking some little resolution that flows directly from the topic of our meditation, some little isolated act or acts that we are going to do that day. But while there is nothing to prevent this, we must not lose sight of our main objective in these daily resolutions. Our main objective is to overcome our predominant fault. If we had a boat in the river, there would be little sense spending our time on holidays polishing the brass rails and the lanterns, to make it look nice, if there was a hole in the bottom of the boat. Sometimes in the spiritual order we can spend time striving for "decorative" virtues that we would like to have or that would make us look good, while we neglect the disastrous hole in the bottom of the boat: our predominant fault.[7] So, other

[7] Just as it is not so pleasant or glamorous to work in the oily bilge, fixing the bottom of the boat, so it is not so pleasant to concentrate on those fundamental faults and vices we have, as is striving to practice some of the more glamorous

resolutions may be auxiliary, but we must remember that we cannot hope to accomplish anything with scatter shots — taking a resolution today about charity, tomorrow humility, the next day simplicity, the next day neatness, and the next day prudence. When we do that, we are practicing everything and learning nothing. So, our daily resolution should be about our particular practice or predominant fault, and it can flow very easily from any topic of meditation.

Further, it is a good thing, particularly in the beginning of our spiritual life, to write down our resolution in a little book or on a scrap of paper. When we have written it down, we have challenged ourselves psychologically, and when the time comes to keep the resolution, we have that added power of recall because of the added sense perception involved in writing and seeing our resolution written and the stimulus it gives when we are tempted not to keep it throughout the day. At the end of the day, we can tear up what we have written or save it in a little book for later reference.

All this, then, in broad, bold strokes is what mental prayer is. It is the use of our mental faculties, our imagination and memory, to aid us to have ideas with our minds, to have thoughts about God, or about some attribute of God, or some virtue in the life of our Lord or the saints. And the purpose of thinking the thoughts is to move our will to make acts — acts of love, faith, hope, contrition, sorrow, and adoration, acts made in our own words, whether expressed or not.

virtues we fancy ourselves to possess. But it is essential to work on those faults.

A Handbook of Spiritual Perfection

It is important to note that these acts need not at all be felt; they have only to be made and to be *meant* with our will. That is the important thing. The less we feel like making them, the more valuable they are in the eyes of God, if we force ourselves to make them. This is so because then we are praying, not for the satisfaction we are receiving, but simply because God wants us to be praying to Him; we are praying to Him with our will, not to please us but to please Him. When it is the greatest struggle, our prayer is most valuable! Always remember that only one failure is possible in spiritual life, and that is to stop trying.

In this chapter, we have been discussing in particular the *what* and the *why* of the process of talking with God, which is called *mental prayer*. We now move on to treat in greater detail the *means* of mental prayer, or *how* to talk with God.

Chapter 3

✤

Talk to God
in mental prayer

The very first step, one that would hardly seem to need pointing out as a means for mental prayer, is the necessity for preparation. "Before you pray," says the Holy Spirit, "prepare thy
soul and be not as the man who tempts God."[8]

Suppose we were about to ask someone for a momentous
favor. We would not suddenly dash right in and blurt out our
request for permission. No doubt we would think about how
we could best present our case, the best reasons we could offer
as to why this favor should be granted, and the strongest motives to move the person we are asking to grant it.

The same planning and preparation are necessary for success in mental prayer. We should think beforehand of whom
we are about to speak to; of what a tremendous privilege it is
that God permits us to speak to Him in prayer any time we
want. If He allowed us to pray to Him only once a week or
once a month, it would be an invaluable favor. But instead,
He permits us to pray to Him any time we want. For that reason, and because what we have to pray for is so important, our
prayer is deserving of very careful preparation.

[8] Ecclus. 18:23 (RSV = Sir. 18:23).

❧

You must have a prayerful disposition

Now, preparation for mental prayer is customarily divided into remote and proximate preparation.

Remote preparation for prayer consists, among other things, in our having habitually the proper dispositions conducive to prayer.

• *Humility.* One of these, and perhaps the most important, is the disposition of humility. We must have some degree of humility if we are going to have any success in mental prayer or in exercising the functions of our soul in a prayerful way. We must have sufficient humility not to brood over real or imagined injuries or slights.

Furthermore, we must have sufficient humility not only not to brood over them, but also to be willing to *forgive* them. We have to make up our mind that if we are going to nurse within our heart antipathies, dislikes, or imagined or real injuries, we are never going to have much success in mental prayer, for those very things and not the thought of God will come into our mind every time we have a quiet moment. The Devil will see to it.

So often we rehearse all the slights and slurs that were said or done to us; we recall what we should have said, and resolve what we will do and say the next time it happens. Such an attitude suffocates the flame of love of God in meditation. Therefore, the first part of the remote preparation for mental prayer consists in trying to acquire some degree of humility.

• *Fidelity to God's will.* The next fundamental disposition that could be considered part of remote preparation for mental prayer is a habitual fidelity to the will of God, especially as His will is manifested to us in the duties of our state in life. If we ever hope to attain any intimacy with God in prayer, which necessarily involves our telling Him that we love Him, since prayer is a relationship of love with God, there cannot be any habitual, deliberate violations of His will.

Remote preparation for mental prayer, then, consists in developing the dispositions proper to prayer, or dispositions of soul that are necessary conditions of prayer; and prominent among these are the dispositions of humility and fidelity to God's will.

⸙

Prepare for each session of mental prayer

The proximate preparation for mental prayer takes place the night before and immediately preceding our meditation in the morning. From our night prayers until we go to sleep, we prepare proximately for our meditation by mulling over, as it were, the topic of meditation, trying to recall what we know about it, what we've heard about it and read about it. We try to plan what we hope to get out of the meditation. In the morning, from the time we rise, we recall our thoughts of the night before. Finally, the immediate preparation consists in acts of faith, adoration, thanksgiving, sorrow, and humility, which we make to enlist God's help in our prayer.

So, preparation for mental prayer consists in disposing ourselves, getting ourselves in condition for prayer both remotely and proximately.

⚓︎

St. Vincent gives you a method for mental prayer

As to the means of making the prayer itself, many of the saints and spiritual writers have devised different and varying methods of mental prayer.

Of all the methods that have been left to us by all the saints, there is none, perhaps, that is more effective and none that is simpler or more logical than the one recommended to us by St. Vincent de Paul. He makes no claim to have originated this method, but we are grateful that in his words and works passed down to us, he has insisted on it so much as a means of meditation for his own religious sons and daughters and also as a means of preaching for his religious sons. It is a method that can be applied to anything that involves the arrangement of ideas; for example, to selling, to giving a talk, to preaching, to writing a composition or essay, or to meditating. It gets simply right at the essence of things.

Perhaps the main phases of St. Vincent de Paul's method of mental prayer can best be demonstrated in action by an example. Suppose the doorbell rang one morning and your mother answered it. A salesman stood at the door holding a large case and asked if he might come in and take a few minutes of her time. She took him into the front parlor, and he opened the case and took out a strange apparatus the like of which she had never seen before. As he deftly assembled it, he began to explain to her its function. It was, as she discovered, a new kind of vacuum cleaner.

He told her and demonstrated to her what the vacuum cleaner would do. "You see, Madam, you don't have to dirty your hands to empty the bag, because it has this disposable bag in it. This attachment is for cleaning the draperies. When you need your upholstery cleaned, you don't have to call someone to take the furniture out of the house, because this nozzle fits right down in back of any chair cushion. With this gadget you clean the radiators. Think, Madam, of the money you spend to have your rugs cleaned each year. Now, we have a simple rug-shampoo device that goes with this machine that will save all that expense. In addition to that, by putting this spray gun to your machine, you can de-moth all your closets." Thus he would go on and tell your mother all about *what* the machine was and *what* it would do — the *nature* of it.

Then, as he could see her admiration of it increasing, he would begin to explain to her *why* she should have it. Think of all the leisure time she would have. Think of all the time she now spends fiddling with that old vacuum cleaner. And fur-thermore, Mrs. Brown next door just purchased one of these new machines and certainly she wouldn't want Mrs. Brown to have something that she did not have.

Perhaps your mother says, "Well, I like it very much, but I'll have to wait until my husband comes home." The salesman has an answer for that! "Well, Madam, what day does your husband stay home and do the housework? I will gladly come and demonstrate it for him; and I know if he saw how much work it was going to save you, he would want you to have it."

Finally, your mother would say, "Well, it really is a wonderful machine. I would love to have it, and I feel sure John would like me to have it, but I don't know how we are ever going to afford it." She doesn't know, but the salesman does! He would be ready at hand to tell her exactly *how* she could acquire it. He would tell her that if she would just put away twenty-five cents a day, give up those weekly movies, and so on, she could easily meet the weekly payments and make a painless acquisition of this new household marvel.

Now, what has the salesman done? First, he told her *what* this beautiful machine is and what it would do for her. Then he told her *why* she should have it. Finally, and most important of all, he very practically got down to brass tacks and told her exactly *how* she could acquire it and make it her own.

That, in a nutshell, is St. Vincent de Paul's method of mental prayer. Three little words characterize it: *what, why,* and *how* — the nature, the motives, and the means. What is the thing, why should I have it, or get rid of it, and how can I do it?

If we remember those three little words — *what, why,* and *how* — we have three hooks on which to hang all our thoughts during meditation. We have the framework on which to build our mental prayer, just like the dress form on which dressmakers fashion a gown. *What* is the thing? If it is a virtue, what is the virtue? What is the nature of it? What does it look like in action? Then, *why* should I have it, if it's a virtue? If it's a vice — pride or unkindness or some other fault — why should I get rid of it? Finally, *how* can I do so? What means can I adopt to enable me to do this?

Talk to God in mental prayer

⚘

Learn how to apply St. Vincent's method

This method can be applied to any subject of meditation conceivable. Suppose, for example, we are meditating on a scene from the life of our Lord. We proceed in the order listed on a theater program. Such a program gives the scene, cast of characters, and the various acts.

So, in meditating on a scene or event in the life of our Lord, we first picture the scene. Perhaps it is our Lord going to Bethany, or returning to Jerusalem, or some other scene from His life. What time in His life was it? His youth, His public life, after His Resurrection? Then we think of the cast of characters. Who was there? The Apostles, our Lord? Any enemies of His? Was Lazarus there? Martha and Mary? Who were the characters? Then we try to recall what they said. What did they do?

All this takes place in and involves using our imagination and our memory. Then, if the meditation is to become practical, we ask what is the lesson in this event for us? What can we learn here from this scene? In any scene from the life of our Lord, we can learn the lesson of almost any virtue — humility, meekness, patience, love. Once we have determined what virtue or what lesson our Lord is teaching us here, we ask ourselves, "What is the *nature* of this lesson or virtue actually? What is it in itself? How is our Lord manifesting it here? Do I know anybody else who manifests it? Do I observe anyone around me who practices this virtue well? *What* is the virtue?"

Then we ask ourselves, "*Why* should I have it? What did our Lord say about it and the necessity of having it? What do

37

the commandments say about it? Is it part of the duties of my state in life?"

Finally, we ask ourselves, "*How* can I get it? First of all, do I have it at all? Do I fail in it? Where do I fail? Oh, yes! That is where I fail the most — in charity. That is the area in which I must do something. Therefore, I will take a resolution about it. I resolve that today, at such-and-such a time, in such-and-such a place, when I am tempted to do such-and-such, I will pray and do the opposite.

That, in brief, is how we use our faculties on our framework: *What* is the thing? *Why* should I have it, or why should I get rid of it? And *how* can I achieve this end?

Do not rely on feelings in prayer

Now, it would not be amiss to mention a few difficulties that we might encounter in the practice of mental prayer. First of all, we should make up our mind never to judge the value of or the effects of our mental prayer by our feelings. Feelings in themselves have nothing to do with its essence or its goodness or badness.

In prayer, there are two possible experiences we can have as far as our feelings are concerned. When we first begin the practice of mental prayer, God sometimes fills us with the greatest kind of consolation, even sensible consolation. We might think, "Oh, how wonderful this is! I'm sorry I wasn't taught all this before. What a wonderful life I have ahead of me. I love this mental prayer!" But suddenly it may happen that God takes away from us all those sensible consolations, all those wonderful feelings, all that apparent ease and facility. Then we begin to wonder what has happened to us because we are not praying anymore.

Here is what has happened: we have been judging the value of our prayer by those pleasurable feelings we had. When the feelings were taken away, we thought the substance of prayer had been lost, which is not true at all.

On the other hand, we may experience none of those warming feelings and consolations. Our prayer might be the driest kind of struggle, like being forced to eat a box of saltines without any water. We might get no satisfaction, no consolation from it at all. But consolation is not the measure of the value of our mental prayer or of the goodness of it. We read of our divine Savior in the Garden that being in agony, He prayed the more.[9] Certainly He was experiencing no pleasure, no consolation in His prayer. Yet who would dare to say that it was not good prayer? That His prayer was good He proved by His conformity to His Father's will.

So too, the effects of our mental prayer and its value and benefit are to be judged, not by our feelings, but by our actions, by what we do. For prayer is the uniting of our minds and will to God. That is why our Lord said, "Pray always."[10] He didn't advise, "Say prayers always," but "Pray always." That is, He told us to have our will and mind united to God always.

When we are engaged in mental prayer, when we are struggling to unite our will to God, not because we enjoy it, but

[9] Cf. Luke 22:43 (RSV = Luke 22:44).
[10] Cf. Luke 18:1; 1 Thess. 5:17.

because we please God thereby, then we are praying. That is His will for us at that time. Therefore, if, independently of our getting any consolation from it, independently of our liking or disliking it, if we go to mental prayer and strive to keep on trying to pray in spite of dryness or distractions, we are praying and our prayer is good.

Remember, the value does not depend on how we feel about it or the satisfaction we get from it. Moreover, the less personal satisfaction we get from our prayer, the more valuable it is likely to be. If we are struggling to pray to please God, and not to please ourselves, if that is why we remain there, then our prayer is all the more valuable because there is no admixture of self-will in it.

Beautiful thoughts are not
the object of mental prayer

Another difficulty must be avoided. We must not fall into the common temptation of beginners and be disturbed by the lack of beautiful thoughts, or what we regard as beautiful or wonderful thoughts. Sometimes we hear people repeat some thoughts that they have had in prayer. Our reaction might be "Glory be to God, how did she ever think of that? I never thought of anything like that; I don't have any thoughts like that!" Well, we must be convinced that having beautiful thoughts or apropos thoughts is not mental prayer. If God does not give us beautiful thoughts, that's all right. They are not the objective of mental prayer. Beautiful thoughts are, in fact, useless unless they achieve their purpose — namely, to stir our wills to make acts of love, adoration, thanksgiving, petition, sorrow, faith, hope, and so on. Thus, let it be clear, the object of mental prayer is not to have lovely thoughts.

Furthermore, for the consolation of beginners, it should be said that the longer we go on in the spiritual life, the more fuel we will have for meditation. As time passes, we shall have done more spiritual reading; we shall have heard more conferences; we shall have studied more about the spiritual life and the nature of the spiritual life. Consequently, we shall have more logs to throw on the blaze in the morning at meditation, fuel with which to stoke the fire of divine love in our heart. Perhaps, at the moment, we are burning twigs and having a hard job scraping them together. But be not disturbed about that, for, as time goes on, we shall have greater and greater sources of fuel, and the woodpile will grow longer and higher.

Always remember that to stir up acts of the will is the objective of the thoughts in mental prayer. The thoughts are useless unless they move us to stir up these acts in our will. St. Vincent de Paul tells us that the considerations, the thoughts in meditation, are like the striking of a match on the flint. The purpose of the striking is to cause the spark that lights the match. But, he says, some people are so foolish as to go on striking the match after it has been lit by continuing to think thoughts and strive for considerations after the will has burst into flames of love. If we are moved to tell God we love Him, or that we are sorry, or any of these acts, we must not think that we have to go back to thinking thoughts because now we are engaged in meditation and should be thinking. No. The purpose of the thoughts is to move us to speak with God. Remember, *that* is our objective.

Therefore, let us not think that we have to be thinking thoughts if our will is speaking to God. The quicker we can get our will speaking to God in familiar conversation, in our own words — the more personal, the better — the better will our mental prayer be. We should strive to talk to God in our own simple, homely, broken English that we use ordinarily. Archbishop Goodier tells us, "I'd rather say, 'Dear God, I love You,' over and over again for an hour, if I could really mean it, than read the most sublime poem by the greatest poet or mystic or saint, the greatest profession of love ever written." Our own words are better. It is *our* love we are giving to God, and we should give it to Him in *our own way*.

We know from reading the account of our Lord's prayer in the Garden that he went back and prayed the "self-same prayer," says St. Matthew, again and again: "Father, if it be possible, let this chalice pass from me; yet not my will but Thine be done."[11]

We read in the life of St. Mary of Egypt,[12] the great penitent, who lived for years in the desert, that she could pray no other prayer than to say over and over again, "Dear Lord, Thou hast made me; now please save me. Thou hast made me; now please save me." This was a perfect prayer, an expression of her utter incapacity and inability to do anything herself and her complete dependence on God, who is all powerful.

[11] Cf. Matt. 26:39, 44; Luke 22:42.
[12] Fifth century.

Talk to God in mental prayer

༺

You must also listen to God in prayer

Because we have stressed talking to God in our own words, with our will, we must not therefore think that we have to do all the talking during mental prayer. It is a conversation with God, not a monologue. Some of the time we should listen! Somebody has said that prayer is not like a game of golf, in which one person hits the ball and then walks to catch up with it and hits it again. It is rather like a game of tennis, in which the ball is hit back and forth, from one contestant to the other. So, while making acts of love, sorrow, petition, faith, and so on, we should do a little listening.

Again, even when we are not listening, it is not necessary to be talking all the time during mental prayer. If we have just told our Lord that we love Him, we can bask in that sentiment. We don't have to keep repeating "I love You, I love You, I love You," like a broken record. We can coast along for a while. We should listen a bit, because God will surely have something to say to us. He is likely to be saying: "If you really love me, you would be doing such-and-such, or you would not be doing such-and-such." We must give Him a chance to say what He has to say to us, for in this way we discover His will for us.

So, our aim in mental prayer is to make acts with our will. But these acts do not have to be incessant. Persevere in a sentiment of love when you have expressed it. The same is true of sentiments or acts of sorrow, contrition, petition, faith, or hope. Coast along in the sentiment until, like a youngster on a scooter, you begin to slow down almost to a stop. Then, to give ourselves more momentum, make another act of whatever it is you are making. When you have given yourself another push, go along with that until you begin to slow to a stop again, and then repeat the process.

Don't be disturbed by distractions

As far as distractions and mental prayer are concerned, we have to make up our minds that it is not easy to fight them. They are something that human flesh is heir to and, like the poor, will be with us always. Sometimes they come from fatigue. Let's face it, meditation is sometimes going to be a battle against fatigue. As long as we don't make peace with fatigue, settle ourselves into a comfortable position, and give up, we need not worry. Making peace with fatigue is the ruination of prayer or the spirit of prayer. But the very struggling against fatigue in prayer to please God is prayer itself, because our will is united to His. Why are we struggling against the fatigue? Only in order to please God, and not ourselves, and that is praying!

A further point might still be made about distractions. Unfortunately, we take the same tools with us to mental prayer that we use all day long. The same mind that we use throughout the course of the day is the mind that we use in mental prayer. Thus, if we are accustomed to let our mind flitter like a bee or a butterfly from blossom to blossom, to any thought that happens to come across it throughout the day, without any attempt at recollection or control of our minds, we cannot hope to expect that for half an hour at meditation it is certainly going to be a very tractable instrument, completely at our command. If a mother has brought up a child who is unmanageable, intractable, and selfish, who has her own way at every moment throughout the course of the day, then, when company comes some Sunday evening, the mother can't expect that spoiled child suddenly to become a docile little model whom the company will admire. It just doesn't happen that way. So, too, with our mind. If it is habitually unstable and uncontrolled throughout the day, if we make no attempt at recollection, no attempt at controlling our thoughts, we cannot expect much success at controlling that mind during our meditation.

Be that as it may, if we find that we have distractions, there is only one thing to do: come back to our prayer. But perhaps we find from experience that when we do pull ourselves back, we are back for thirty seconds and then we are off again. In that case, there is only one course of action. As soon as we are conscious again that we are away, we must come back! Involuntary distractions do not hinder the fruits of our prayer, either mental prayer or vocal prayer. As long as they are involuntary, as long as we are doing what we can to avoid them, we need not worry. The problem with distractions is not so much how to avoid them, as how to make them involuntary.

Each time we find we are distracted, we must try gently to come back. If we find that we can't do anything else, let us talk to God about the distractions: "You know, dear Lord, I'd like to be thinking about what I should be thinking about. I'd like to be thinking about You. But I just can't seem to keep my mind on it. You know how weak I am. You must help me; this can't go on." In this way, we tell God we want to think of Him and ask Him to accept the distraction as prayer. Perhaps that is all we have to offer Him. We haven't any beautiful thoughts. So we ask Him to take this distraction as our offering for this day. In other words, we try to turn our very distraction into a prayer.

The thing to keep in mind about mental prayer, then, is that as long as we are trying, we are praying, and that is the important thing. What leads to discouragement is the thought that we are wasting our time. But there is never a waste of time if we are trying. It is only when we settle back and give up that we waste our time. As long as we are trying, we are bending our wills to God. We are praying whenever we keep tirelessly turning ourselves back from every distraction, when we keep on making the effort in spite of lack of satisfaction.

Again, let it be said, there is only one failure possible throughout the whole spiritual life, and particularly in the sphere of mental prayer, and that is to stop trying.

Chapter 4

✌

Identify your predominant fault

It cannot be emphasized too often that love of God — perfection, holiness, sanctity — consists in the union of our will with God's will, and that means an active and passive union. That is to say that loving God means that we do all we know He wants us to do, and that we want all that He does to us or wills to happen to us. The only obstacle to perfection, to holiness, to sanctification, to love of God, to union with God, is the thing called *sin*, the essence of which is the *lack* of conformity of our will with God's will — or, in other words, the opposition of our will to God's will. Wherever we have opposition between our will and God's will, whether it be grave opposition or mediocre or slight opposition, to that extent we are imperfect; to that extent we are failing to love God as completely as He wants us to.

From this fact arises the necessity of knowing ourselves, of seeing the deformity between our will and God's will. It is necessary to *know* this deformity in order to correct it. In other words, to be completely pleasing to God, it is necessary to know ourselves and to know wherein we depart from God's will. Hence, the necessity of knowing our sins and our faults, of knowing our failings, frailties, and, above all, our habitual tendencies. Shadowboxing never produced a knockout. Neither can we fight an unknown or invisible enemy.

But the knowledge of our predominant faults is not the easiest knowledge in the world to come by, despite the proximity of its source. In fact, the very nearness of the object makes it more difficult to see. Others we know better than ourselves. If we had to write two essays, one describing our own faults, and the other those of our neighbor, we would probably score a higher grade for our analysis of our neighbor than of ourselves. It is much easier to know a companion's faults than our own. After all, we feel the effects of her faults, whereas we don't very often feel the effects of our own. We can diagnose and prescribe for her failings with assurance. Yet the most important knowledge in the world for us or any individual is the knowledge of ourselves: "Know thyself."

Actually, we do not really know ourselves until we are ready to say at any moment, "This is my predominant fault; this is the thing that I need most to work on; this is the failing that is standing most in the way of my being fully committed to our Lord; this is the trait that others find most difficult in me; this is the characteristic that makes me hardest to live with; this is the habit that most needs correction; this is the tendency that spawns most of my difficulties." How few there are who can say that on call!

Your self-knowledge must be precise

But knowing our predominant fault involves more than being able to name it. We must be aware of the particular form it takes, that is, the characteristic way in which it manifests itself. Defective or inaccurate knowledge here explains not only much abandoned effort, but also much omitted effort. After lack of motivation, of which we spoke in the first chapter, fuzziness about its manifestations is probably the most common cause of scant progress in fighting a predominant fault.

Suppose we are asked, "What is your predominant fault?" Would we reply vaguely, "I dunno; pride, I guess." Or would we say confidently, "That's easy. Pride!" Before we gloat, learn that *both* those answers, the befuddled and the certain one, reveal no more precise information than did a certain South American amnesiac in the play *Charlie's Aunt*. Someone asked what part of Brazil she lived in. Her uninformative reply was "The residential part!" It is equally unrevealing to catalog our predominant fault simply as pride. Such a skimpy symptom gives a spiritual surgeon an almost hopeless task in planning the proper prescription. Why? Because *every* fault and every sin has its root in pride and is in some way a manifestation of pride, just as every act of virtue is, in some way, a manifestation of charity.

Who can count the ways in which pride can rear its ugly head? For example, one list of examination-of-conscience questions has no fewer than 207 manifestations of pride as a predominant fault. They range from "Have I a superior attitude in thinking, or speaking, or acting?" all the way to the opposite end of the gamut: "Do I think or speak or act timidly?" Presumably the writer of that list does not pretend to have exhausted all the possible manifestations of pride. No spiritual author would be so proud as to claim that! So, "My predominant fault is pride" is a clumsy phrase that indicates but does not reveal.

The same lack of precision must be avoided in thinking of a particular virtue we might have as a spiritual practice. To be proper, sensible, and practical, it must be defined. It must be limited to and pinpointed to a workable, achievable goal. To say that our practice is charity is much too broad. We say our predominant fault is against charity, but what phase of charity? How does our fault against charity manifest itself? Is it by stubbornness? Or failure to conform to the wishes of the group? Is it against charity in speech? Charity in thought? Criticism? We must pin it down until we know precisely what our predominant fault is.

Only then can we work on it sensibly and systematically. Since our faults crop up in so many diverse forms, small wonder that unenlightened struggling against them is often as frustrating as trying to nail a custard pie to the wall. Hence, we abandon the struggle almost before it begins.

A successful campaign against a predominant fault, then, in addition to proper motivation, demands a clear-cut knowledge of the objective, seeing as clearly as possible the nature of our predominant fault and its particular form of manifestation. The more clearly we are able to isolate it, the greater the chances of success in the battle.

You can learn from God what your predominant fault is
But how can we identify our faults and our failings or sins? Above all, how can we discover our predominant fault? Well,

there are three sources of knowledge. First, we can learn about it by a special illumination from God. Some special actual grace, something we read, something that we hear or see can suddenly make us realize, "My glory, I've been doing that for years and never recognized it or was never conscious of it." This sudden inspiration is a light from God. If He did not send us special lights in prayer to illumine us as to our carelessness in His service, we would never travel very far along the road to perfection. One shaft of His divine light cast into our souls in prayer will illumine us as to our imperfections more than twenty lifetimes of conscience-examining would do, just as one suffering sent by God will reveal more to us about our self-love and will healingly hurt our pride more than a thousand years of our own carefully thought-out and self-chosen penances would.

These split-second revelations of God's wisdom flash into our soul only when it is in the quiet of prayer and not moving about with its own activity and imaginations and human reasoning.

Others can show you your predominant fault

In spite of these revelations from God, we can never be excused from the personal effort involved in seeking to discover by ourselves our predominant fault. Barring God's making it known by a special illumination, two methods are at hand: learn it from others, or search it out ourselves.

The first way is to learn it from others — a painful process indeed. So, here tread lightly! Unless we have a sincere desire to be better, self-knowledge acquired from others is only an irritant. Criticism always smarts. We spontaneously resent being accused. Yet, in spite of this, criticism often points most surely to our failings. By nature we judge ourselves more kindly than others do. We don't have to be taught to overlook faults in ourselves that we bitterly condemn in others. We excuse ourselves, accuse others. They do the same.

Further, faults that we often do not even suspect in ourselves are so evident to others that they assume we must know them. Thus, they freely speak of them. Hence, if we are sincere, if we are looking for the truth, there is rare opportunity to discover it in the criticism of others. We need only be willing to shake off the sting and look for it.

Too often, we don't. We find a million excuses why this act of ours was really not a fault in us, even though it might appear so to our neighbor. We say to ourselves or to others, "I wouldn't mind if it were true, but this criticism is so wrong. Anything but that!" An observation: the criticism that stings the most is probably the one that touches the rawest wound. Look at it closely!

So, the first source of clues in tracking down a predominant fault is the criticisms, corrections, or admonitions of others, whether they be dealt to us directly and in person or received "behind our back," so to speak, from meddling or subversive companions. A person who is seriously interested in learning his predominant fault and its more subtle manifestations will examine and analyze diligently the probable justification for any criticism or correction he has received. It may be the missing clue to his predominant fault.

Identify your predominant fault

You can discover your predominant fault yourself

Apart from others' stunning us with the knowledge of our predominant fault, we have the alternative of digging it out ourselves. In spite of the essentially do-it-yourself character of discovering our predominant fault, we normally get assistance from our confessor or spiritual director. This happens after we have discussed ourselves with him and made known what we regard as our predominant failure, the one that hinders most our full commitment to our Lord.

Our purpose in striving to isolate this predominant fault is based on the long-successful military tactic "divide and conquer." When we are best concentrating our reforming efforts on one particular fault at a time, we gain greater victories than by flailing wildly at too many objectives at once. Such scatter-shooting takes very much trouble to make very little progress. This is noteworthy because a similar principle serves well in actually segregating a predominant fault. This principle is "divide and discover."

To make this clear, imagine a housewife losing the diamond from her ring in a barrel of flour. Her furious fumbling in the flour up to her shoulder might never discover the jewel. The whitened tips of her probing fingers might tantalizingly graze the stone a dozen times, and she would never realize it. Her best course is to empty the barrel of flour into small piles and sift them, bit by bit, until she has isolated the missing diamond.

So, too, in seeking a hidden predominant fault. We must try to separate into small categories or divisions all the actions and endurings of our life and the motives that underlie them. We must try to isolate the missing or unknown stone that is our predominant fault from all the other actions and motives and impulses in which it lies hidden, doing its subversive work. We must divide to discover.

But suppose that in our search, several faults stare us in the conscience. Any one of them merits a lifetime of work, and all of them seem predominant. We are not able to decide which one is the most predominant, or which needs working on first. What are we to do? What hierarchical order must be observed in the attack?

In this case, the principle of "divide and discover" must be applied still further.

- *Sin confessed most often.* In determining the most spiritually profitable fault on which to work, we are abetted by questioning ourselves: "What do I confess the most?" A review of our confessions during the past year should produce fruitful results. Certainly frequent confession properly integrated into our spiritual life will or should contain an avowal of progress or failure in the struggle against the predominant fault. If we don't tell our predominant fault, what do we confess?

- *Coldest, most deliberate sin.* Now, among those sins confessed regularly, choose the one, if any, that is, most *coldly deliberate* — that you know you commit, yet knowingly resist God's grace given to avoid it, time after time. Again, between two faults, assuming similar frequency, choose first the graver one to work on.

♦ *Sin committed most often.* Again, among habitual sins, presuming similar gravity, choose the one *you do more often,* the one for which you have the strongest affection. The reason is that, allowed to continue unimpeded, the habit only digs in more solidly; you acquire a greater affection for the forbidden action. Thus the *Imitation* says, "Resist at first, lest the evil gather strength by longer delay."[13]

♦ *External sin.* Pursuing further the process of "divide and discover," we must consider additional basic principles that will affect the choice we must inevitably make of a predominant fault. Between an external and internal fault, presuming similar gravity, choose the *external* to work on first. The reason is that the external fault has the added gravity of scandal, or bad example, or perhaps affects our neighbor in an even more direct way, and thus violates charity. "The greatest of these is charity."[14]

♦ *Sin against obedience or abandonment.* If there are no outstanding faults against charity, choose the one against obedience, that is, the failure against the active phase of holiness — namely, doing what God wants. If there are none, then look for the one against abandonment, the passive part of holiness — namely, wanting what God does.

[13] Thomas à Kempis, *Imitation of Christ,* Bk. 1, ch. 13, no. 4.
[14] 1 Cor. 13:13.

⁂

Find your root fault

A further concept remains to be established as a guide in determining our predominant passion or fault and, consequently, our spiritual practice and the subject of our particular examen.[15] We must beware of the fallacious practice of treating a rash on the surface while overlooking or failing to remove the cancerous growth within our heart and will that is causing the surface blemish. It is very possible to treat one rash after another without ever really attacking the cause.

In speaking of this subject, St. Francis de Sales says, "Our examination of conscience must be reduced to a search for our passions. For so far as examination for sins is concerned, that is for the confessions of those who are not trying to advance. What affections are a hindrance to our heart, what passions are in possession of it, in what does it chiefly go astray? For it is by the passions of the soul that one gets to know one's state, by probing them one after the other."[16]

What St. Francis refers to as *passion* is what we mean by root faults, or faults from which other faults flow — capital sins, as it were. What he is telling us in effect is that it is more important to discover what we *are* than what we do.

For example, suppose we think that our predominant fault is impatience. The impatience may be only the rash on the

[15] The examen is a daily examination of conscience performed to root out sin. See Chapter 5.

[16] St. Francis de Sales (1567-1622; Bishop of Geneva), *Introduction to the Devout Life*, Pt. 5, ch. 7.

surface. Why do we become impatient? If we analyze it, it is because things do not go as we want them to. Hence, the real underlying fault or passion in this case is attachment to our own will. That, then, should be uppermost in our mind when we are resolving to combat temptations against patience. It should make us alert to other subtle manifestations of attachment to our own will.

Again, suppose we think our predominant fault is criticism. The criticism very likely is only a rash on the surface. Why are we critical? Of whom? Is it not because we have an antipathy toward the one or the ones we criticize? Hence, the real passion, the real basic fault we should be conscious of as we fight the criticism is hatred or antipathy.

By discovering and attacking our root fault, we are able to combat many of its manifestations at the same time. There are two ways of shutting off a lawn sprinkler. We can fight our way to the sprinkler head and try to plug each tiny spray hole with a toothpick, and get plenty wet in the process. Or we can walk calmly to the other end of the hose and turn off the tap that is feeding water to all the little holes. Concentrating on multiple outward manifestations of our predominant fault is like plugging the little holes in the sprinkler head instead of going straight to the basic vice that is the source of the outward faults.

Holiness calls you to do what God wants
and to want what He wants

Up to this point, general means and principles have been pointed out for discovering our predominant fault. It is time to descend to some particularized aids for more sharply focusing our predominant failure within our view. By way of introducing them, let it be repeated that all of holiness and perfection and sanctity consists of union of our will with the will of God. But this union with God's will, like a medal, has two sides or aspects, one active, the other passive. Active union with God's will means doing what God wants. Passive union with God's will means wanting all that God does. Any notion of holiness or perfection that does not consider both its active and passive aspects is gravely deficient.

The active and passive side of holiness are symbolized most beautifully by the front and back of the Miraculous Medal, which Mary revealed to the humble Daughter of Charity St. Catherine Labouré.[17] On the front of the medal, a burst of dazzling, luminous rays streaming from Mary's hands illumines the path ahead like a floodlight, showing us what God wants us to do — the active part of holiness. On the back, the sword-pierced, thorn-crowned immaculate hearts of Mary and her Son, surmounted by the Cross, recall vividly their wanting what God does, the patient acceptance of all He sends, which is the passive part of holiness.

Studying the two sides of the Miraculous Medal in the light of the two aspects of holiness they signify provides the two broadest and most obvious categories in which we can seek our predominant fault. Ultimately, any predominant fault will be opposed to one or the other phase of perfection, the active or the passive. Either we will fail actively to do what God

[17] 1806-1876.

wants — namely, against obedience or charity, shown by preferring our own will to His will; or we will fail passively to want
what God does — namely, against abandonment to His will,
shown by rebelling against what He wills for us. In these three
virtues — obedience, charity, and abandonment — can be
conveniently summed up our whole duty toward God and our
neighbor.

*You may have a predominant
fault against obedience*

Thus, we could begin our search for our predominant fault
in no better way than by asking ourselves whether it trans-
gresses the active aspect of loving God, that is, doing what He
wants; or whether it fails in the passive aspect of loving God,
that is, wanting what He does.

First, mindful of the front of the Miraculous Medal and
Mary's rays showing the way, symbolizing the active phase of
holiness, let us consider some common external manifestations of a fundamental fault of preferring our own will to God's
will for us in the specific matter of obedience. Such manifestations could be slothfulness and unpunctuality. Our fault might
be slothfulness in rising, slothfulness in our duty, slothfulness
in our prayers. It might be unpunctuality, the habit of constantly being late, dragging up the rear, rushing to get in line.
It might be delay in stopping our duty, or whatever else we
might be doing, at the proper time.

Still further surface rashes of the cancer of self-will in the
sphere of obedience might appear in the form of criticalness of

authority, criticalness of order, and criticalness of things we are asked to do.

⚓

You may have a predominant
fault against charity

Let us look now for a moment at some particular manifestations of preferring our own will to God's will for us in the matter of charity. Do we find ourselves speaking of the faults of others habitually, speaking disparagingly of them? Do we remember that every time we have finished speaking of anybody, we have spread peace or war, love or hate, Heaven or Hell? Do we think that somebody else is better respected or regarded because of what we have said about them, or less respected and regarded?

Again, are we morose and habitually sad, or too serious, or a gloom spreader, walking around with a face that looks like the back wheels of a hearse? Are we slovenly in our person, in our dress, in the way we do our work or our duty, or in the way we keep our desk, all of which are subtle manifestations of lack of consideration and esteem for our neighbor?

Is our characteristic fault a certain stubbornness, wanting our own way, wanting things done the way we want them? Are we rigid, unbending, unwilling to give and take, criticizing mentally or verbally those who do not do things the way we would want them done?

Again, in the realm of charity, do we deliberately entertain aversions? True, we can't help feeling aversions. But we can control and avoid manifesting them. Furthermore, experience proves and faith teaches that if we pray hard enough and want it hard enough, God can bring it about that we don't even feel them anymore.

⚭

Your predominant fault may be a
failure to want what God wants

So much for some sample indications of preferring to do our own will over God's will in the spheres of obedience and charity. There remains now to recall the love-wounded hearts on the reverse of the Miraculous Medal, calling to mind the passive aspect of holiness, and to explore, at least superficially, manifestations of a very prevalent root fault — namely, failure to want what God does, failure to conform our will to what He sends us. We are speaking of faults that come under the heading of rebellion against God's will, or the opposite of the virtue of abandonment to the will of God.

Are we habitually irritable when things happen that we do not want, when we are crossed and fail to get what we want? Do we show our irritability? Are we always whining and complaining about the way things are and asking why they are not different? Is this because things are not to our liking? Do we manifest a lack of meekness in our temper when things go wrong? Do others know about it from the explosion when we make a mistake?

Again, is our fault oversensitiveness? Do we regard every little oversight, every little act of thoughtlessness, as some kind of insult or offense to us and give way to sadness and weeping because we have been slighted and overlooked?

Do we give in to excessive discouragement when our work fails or when we don't seem to improve? All of these faults are manifestations of our disposition of rebellion against God, whose Providence extends to everything that happens to us without exception.

All of the potential, predominant tendencies and faults of our character that manifest themselves externally, which we have been discussing, are the type of thing that we should mention in speaking of ourselves with our director, confessor, or superior for the purpose of determining our spiritual practice.

Chapter 5

❧

Learn to root out
your faults

❧

Once we have discovered, with consultation, our predominant fault, it remains to attack it by making it the matter of our particular examination. Actually, there are two kinds of examination of conscience, one called the *general examen*, and the other, the *particular examen*.

The general examen is a brief retrospect of our whole day — spiritual, mental, and physical — that is made during our night prayers. It is a backward glance over the day, adding up the debits and credits, seeking to discover how we have performed our spiritual exercises, how we have done our work, how we have lived our life. The point to remember about the general examen is that its purpose is not merely to discover our faults, but to tell God that we are sorry for them and to ask His help to avoid them the following day.

The particular examen, with which we are immediately concerned, takes place twice a day, generally at midday and in the evening. It concentrates, not on all of our actions of the morning or of the afternoon, but upon some particular, specific virtue that we are trying to acquire, or some particular, specific vice or fault that we are trying to overcome. This is known as our spiritual practice, or simply our practice.

Concentrating our efforts and attention on one particular fault or virtue at the particular examen has many advantages. First, it helps us realize the fault more clearly. We have an opportunity twice a day to reaffirm our determination to overcome this particular fault and to renew our petitions to God to give us the help we need to overcome it.

In addition to this, because we have isolated it, our attention can focus more clearly on it and we can estimate our progress better. We are like a woman buying a set of draperies. She goes into a drapery store and is confused by the mass of colors and patterns as she sees them all hanging together. So, she takes the pair in which she is interested over to the window, where she can see them in the daylight, away from the distraction of all the other colors. She can make a better choice then; she can picture how they are going to look in the situation in which she wants them. She focuses her attention on them better.

The same principle explains the meaningfulness and importance of the particular examen. Twice a day we take the occasion to examine ourselves on how we have done with our practice, that is, the particular virtue we are trying to acquire or the vice we are trying to overcome. We consider that virtue or vice in itself, exclusive of other faults we might have or virtues we might be seeking.

It can be a difficult thing to remain attentive during and carry out well the exercise of the particular examen, even though it lasts only about a minute. Admittedly there are many difficulties attached to making our particular examen. Many reasons conspire to produce this hardship.

First, the very time of the day at which it is to be made con-tributes to its difficulty. After the burden and heat of the morn-ing or the afternoon, our mind is prone to be cluttered with distractions, not the least of which might be our wondering what we are going to have for our meal, which is imminent.

The only answer to the difficulty of time is to face it squarely and motivate ourselves properly. Nothing worthwhile is ever accomplished without effort. If we see the examen in its proper perspective as a worthwhile, necessary, and desirable goal, we will pray and make the effort to carry it out well in spite of the difficulties and distractions.

But even greater obstacles than distractions can prevent us from making the particular examen well, if at all. One of these is the failure to take a definite and workable resolution about our practice or predominant fault in our meditation. Another obstacle is the lack of any method or plan for making the par-ticular examen itself.

ço

Your resolutions should be particular

First, let it be said that the whole success of a particular examen will depend on the kind of resolution we take in the morning at our meditation. The very purpose of the particular examen is to see whether we kept our resolution about our practice. As was emphasized when speaking about the resolu-tion in the chapter on mental prayer, it must be particular if it is to be worthwhile at all.

For example, it profits nothing to say, "Today I resolve to be charitable," or, "Today I resolve to be better," or, "Today I resolve to be patient." We are wasting our breath on such generic resolutions, and we might as well save it for something useful. Unless we specify and particularize and challenge ourselves with the details of the resolution, we won't succeed in carrying it out.

So, no matter what virtue we are practicing, or what fault we are trying to overcome, we must try to foresee at meditation, if we can, the precise time today we are likely to be tempted in this way. In the case of overcoming a fault, we must, in formulating our resolution, ask ourselves when we are likely to be uncharitable, in what place, and under what circumstances? Or when are we likely to be tempted to entertain this antipathy, or to be impatient, or to be proud, or to be stubborn, or to be anything else? Is it after breakfast? Is it while we are doing our work? Is it in class? When is it? If we are able to pinpoint it, that is the time we should resolve about: "At eight o'clock this morning, during my chores, or at ten o'clock in my office, or at eleven o'clock in class, when I am tempted to do such-and-such, I resolve to . . ." But what do we resolve to do?

⋙

Your resolutions should be positive

Right here, let us not make the mistake of resolving that we won't be impatient, we won't be unkind, we won't entertain that jealousy or antipathy, or we won't be stubborn. In the first place, that is not resolving to do something, but resolving *not* to do something. And *not* acting is always weaker and less effectual than acting.

In the second place, it smacks of the kind of resolution St. Peter took in all his pride and impetuousness. "Even though they all deny you, I will not deny you."[18] We know, of course, that before the day was over, St. Peter had fallen on his face. That was because he trusted in himself and his own strength and efforts. We must not repeat his mistake.

Our resolution should always manifest trust in God and mistrust in ourselves. Our Lord said, "Without me, you can do nothing."[19] He did not say we could do a little bit, but He said, "Without me you can do nothing." Therefore, our resolution should always be to *do* something, and the something we should resolve to do is *pray*, to call upon God's help *during* temptation. The most important time to pray is in the midst of the temptation, at the height of the attack by the enemy. If we should not call for reinforcements against the enemy at that time, when should we do so?

Therefore, no matter what fault we are trying to overcome, our resolution during morning prayers will always be to pray during temptation. Hence, our resolution will run like this: "This morning, at eight o'clock, when I will be tempted to give So-and-so a sharp answer, I will pray such-and-such a prayer." Furthermore, right then and there at meditation time, we should determine precisely which prayer or aspiration we will say during temptation that day. Perhaps it will be a prayer we will make up ourselves. Perhaps it will be an invocation selected from a litany. No matter. The important thing is to

---

[18] Cf. Mark 14:29.
[19] John 15:5.

select the prayer and determine to say it when we are tempted to commit our predominant fault.

⚜

Your resolutions will prepare
you to face temptation

But there is yet a step further to go in formulating our resolution, which can be made clear in this manner: all the process of devising our resolution bears a striking analogy to a fire drill. The purpose of a fire drill is to predetermine, in the calmness of a non-emergency situation, precisely what is to be done when an emergency does break out. The exits are located, an escape path is plotted, the location of the alarm box is noted, and the fire extinguishers are spotted. If we waited until the confusion of a conflagration was rampant before trying to decide what to do or how to escape, disaster would follow.

♦ *Determine what to do during temptation.* So, taking a resolution at morning meditation is our daily fire drill. In the calm of a non-emergency situation at prayer, we plan precisely what we will do when the fire of temptation breaks out. It is morally certain to break out, since we are concerned with temptations to our predominant fault. If we wait until the blaze has burst upon us to think of what we should do, disaster will follow, as so many of our charred experiences of the past can testify.

Hence the necessity of knowing, as precisely as we can, exactly what we should do when the fire of temptation begins to scorch us and singe the hairs on our

hands and eyebrows. Hence, too, the importance of determining the precise prayer we will say, that is, the exact fire extinguisher we will use.

• *Pray until the temptation has passed.* All of this brings us
to the further step in our resolution formation alluded
to above. We resolved to say such-and-such a prayer at
the time of temptation. But how many times will we say
that prayer on the occasion of that temptation? Would
we say it once or twice and then give in to the temptation? How long would we squirt a fire extinguisher on a
fire? Obviously, until the fire was out. So, too, we should
resolve to say our selected prayer over and over until
the fire of temptation is overcome or under control.

• *Motivate yourself to carry out your resolution.* The final
step of the resolution is to propose to ourselves a supernatural motive for carrying out our resolution. Why are
we going to be on the alert for temptation so that we
may pray all during it? To please God, to show our love,
or to make reparation. Some such supernatural motive
should be proposed to ourselves.

• *Assign yourself a penance to do if you fail to carry out
your resolution.* Then, if we really mean that we are going to do this for the sake of God, and if we are truly serious about it, we will add to our resolution this codicil:
"If I fail to do this, I will do or omit such-and-such a
thing as a penance to myself." But if we decide to assign
ourselves a penance, it should be sufficiently difficult to

be a deterrent to us at the time of temptation. In other words, we would rather overcome the temptation than do the penance. A suggestion: How about memorizing three verses of Scripture as a penance each time we fail to keep our resolution?

Now, one by one, we have accumulated all the elements of a good resolution: we have tried to foresee the time, the place, the circumstances, the action we will do, and the motive. Putting them all together, we have a resolution like this: This morning, at eight o'clock, when my coworker Bob comes into my office and starts boasting about his promotion and poking fun at my job, and I am tempted to tell Bob what I think of him, I will say, "Virgin most prudent, pray for me," and I will say it over and over until I have conquered the temptation. I am going to do this to show my love for You, dear Lord.

Now, if we take resolutions that are particularized like that, much of the difficulty of the particular examen will disappear.

Learn the method for the particular examen

If we are formulating proper resolutions in the morning, we have but to follow this very simple and effective method for a most successful particular examen.

The first thing is to be recollected and ask God for the grace to make the examen well. Then, since the purpose of the particular examen is to check on our progress against our particular fault or in our special virtue — in a word, our prac-tice — we don't have to bother tediously going over our whole morning's activities. Instead, we mentally go right to the heart of the matter. What was our resolution this morning? It concerned eight o'clock. Did I say that prayer over and over when I was tempted to be antagonistic? No matter what our resolution might have been, I ask, "Did I say that prayer that I said I was going to say when I was tempted to be impatient, or to think those uncharitable thoughts, or to indulge that antipathy? Did I say the prayer?" If we did, we know it immediately. If we did not, we likewise know it immediately. The particular examen is over as far as that point is concerned. It wasn't so difficult to make after all, was it?

Then, if we find we have kept our resolution, we say, "Thank You, dear Lord. I could not have done it without Your help." On the other hand, if we did not keep it, we say, "Dear Lord, I said I was going to do that, and I didn't do it. I'm sorry, but I thank You for the help You gave me, which I didn't use. But this afternoon is going to be better!"

Thus we examine ourselves to see whether we kept our resolution. We thank God if we did, and we thank Him if we did not. Then we renew our resolution for the afternoon. Again, we try to foresee the time and place and circumstances this afternoon in which we are likely to be tempted or have an opportunity to commit this fault. Will it be at a meal? Will it be while I'm doing the dishes? Will it be in class? When will it be? Each of us knows that. So this afternoon, at such-and-such a time, when So-and-so says something, or does something, or when this happens or that happens, and I am tempted to be impatient, to be unkind, to be uncharitable, to entertain this antipathy, or to lose my temper, or whatever my predominant fault is, I will pray such-and-such a prayer, and I will say this prayer over and over again until the temptation has passed.

Then, at the evening particular examen, we simply repeat our process of noontime and renew our resolution for the period after supper until retirement time. At the general examen at night, we take a quick look at our achievement of the evening. So, as has been said before, we have divided the day into three distinct segments with three check-up points.

This is a simple, effective method for the particular examen. What are the steps? Recollection, thinking of what we are going to do; asking God briefly for the grace we need; then going mentally immediately to the time and the place of our particular resolution to see whether we have kept it. It takes but an instant to think of that. Then we thank God for the results or ask His pardon for failure, and renew the resolution for the next period of the day. That is all there is to the exercise of the particular examen, which some regard as so horrendous and difficult.

If we carry out our daily particular examinations in this way, the success or failure we have had all week rightfully becomes the foremost matter we take to our confession. We report on the progress we have made in overcoming our predominant fault or acquiring the virtue we need the most. Thus, there is a sensible unity to our spiritual life. We are not floundering and flailing about like a baby tossed in a swimming pool, just trying to keep our heads above water. Instead, we are going at it sensibly, reasonably, with a definite plan.

The chief matter of our confession, then, will be the virtue or vice about which we are taking our particular resolution, and the fact of whether we are making progress or sliding backward. If this is the case, it is not going to take us a month to examine our conscience every week. If we have been making a particular examen in this fashion every day, twice a day, or three times, we can rightfully spend most of our preparation time for Confession as it should be spent, on arousing sorrow for our sins, not on trying to find them.

≈

Combat interior faults by practicing interior virtues

Up to this point in our discussion of a method for particular examen, we have been stressing the combat against exterior faults in particular. But it is possible that our major fault is interior. It might be an interior fault of pride, of self-complacency, or lack of recollection — dissipation, if you will. It might be a tendency to discouragement.

The way to tackle an interior fault is to resolve to practice the opposite virtue at the time of temptation. It is essentially a positive approach. For example, suppose we have an interior fault of self-complacency, or love of praise and flattery; we preen like a peacock if we hear somebody talk about us or say we did a good job. We habitually refer all our accomplishments to ourselves.

In such a case, we should make a resolution like this: Each time this morning I find myself thinking about myself as something quite wonderful, or hear anybody say anything about me, and I am tempted to be complacent, I will make an act of humility by saying this prayer: "Not to us, O Lord, not to us, but to Thy name give glory,"[20] or, "I refer everything to You; not to me, O Lord, but to You." And I will say this prayer over and over until the temptation has passed.

Or, suppose we have an internal fault of giving way to discouragement. In that event, we can resolve the following: Every time I am tempted to feel discouraged this morning, I am going to make an act of trust in God by saying, "Sacred Heart of Jesus, I place my trust in Thee," or, "Dear Lord, I trust in Thee completely," or, "Lord I do believe; help my unbelief."[21] And I will repeat this prayer over and over until the temptation has passed.

Choose something to remind you often
of your spiritual practice

In addition to using actual temptations as occasions for making these acts, we can choose a reminder for the day or for the week, a reminder to prompt us to make such acts of virtue. For example, we can resolve that every time we walk upstairs this morning we are going to make an act of trust in God; or every time we see this pin in our sleeve, or any time we do anything else, whatever it might be, or any time any particular thing happens, we are going to make an act of trust in God.

The number and kinds of reminders we might choose as prompters to make acts of trust in God within us, or of any interior virtue, are limitless. For example: each time we step on

---

[20] Ps. 113b:1 (RSV = Ps. 115:1).
[21] Mark 9:23 (RSV = Mark 9:24).

an elevator; each time the phone rings; each time someone walks into our office; each time we walk up steps; each time we hear the clock strike; each time we hear a plane fly overhead. A teacher might use as a reminder the act of opening a book in class. She might make a mark on the board, an unobtrusive asterisk, a cross, the initials of a brief prayer. Each time she turned to the board, or saw it from the back of the room, it would remind her to make her act of interior humility or trust, or to recall the presence of God within her, or whatever else her practice might be.

Of course, our reminder is only a reminder *as long as it reminds*. We can get so used to seeing and hearing things in their accustomed place or at their accustomed time that we don't really see or hear them at all. That is, we don't see or hear them until they get out of their accustomed place. For that reason, a very good reminder is to change the position of a statue or crucifix on the desk so that it obtrudes itself on our consciousness. When it does, we are reminded, and we make our act of virtue.

It should be noted that the same kind of familiarity here can likewise vitiate the effectiveness of a chosen prayer or aspiration. After we have said an aspiration many times, over a long period of time, it can become mere mechanical repetition. We might as well be saying, "Atomic Energy Commission, watch over us." An aspiration is important because it directs our mind to God for an instant. If it ceases to do this, it has lost its effectiveness. That is why it is helpful to change our aspiration from time to time. That is why, also, it is helpful sometimes to try to turn our mind to God without saying any words. Then we will be practicing real prayer and really praying. Then we shall be reminded that it is possible to say aspirations without praying, that is, without turning our mind to God; but it is not possible to turn our mind to God without turning our mind to God, that is, without praying.

Having changed our reminder or our prayer, it is possible that familiarity will again vitiate its usefulness. In that case, we should not hesitate to change it again. For some this can or must be done daily; for others it might be necessary only weekly or monthly. The reminder is a tool to help us to attack our interior failing by practicing positively the virtue that is opposed to the failing. Consequently, we must strive to keep our tool sharp and in good condition.

In this method of striving to overcome an interior fault, or to acquire an interior virtue, at the time of particular examen we merely check to see whether we did, in fact, use those temptations as occasions for making acts of our particular virtue, or when we did go upstairs or come in contact with any one of our reminders, whether we did, in fact, make acts of this virtue. Then, we renew our resolution for the afternoon and the evening, as the case may be, as explained above.

You may face unforeseeable temptations
to your predominant fault

Before concluding these suggestions for making our daily resolution and particular examen, it will not be amiss to propose a solution to two possible difficulties that might be experienced in the practical order.

Learn to root out your faults

First, what do we do if, at resolution time at morning meditation, we are honestly unable to foresee precisely any occasion in which we will probably be tempted to our predominant fault? Suppose, for example, our predominant fault is criticism. Conceivably, as we look ahead to our morning, we cannot anticipate any particular occasion that might arise in which we will be tempted to be critical. However, we do know that only a rare morning passes without our being critical in some way. The same thing could be said if our predominant fault were impatience, or surliness, or complaining, or any other.

In such a case, when we cannot foresee all the precise elements of a good resolution — namely, time, place, circumstances, action, and motive — then we can do the next best thing. We can select a definite *time* during which, no matter what we are doing, we will be especially on our guard against that fault. For example, we could resolve: This morning, from eight to nine o'clock in [wherever I customarily am at that hour], I will be particularly watchful for temptations to criticism [or impatience, or surliness or whatever our practice might be].

If we were conversing with a companion as we walked and saw ahead of us on the sidewalk a glassy sheet of ice, we would, as we drew near to it, interrupt our conversation somewhat, if not stop it altogether. Perhaps we would even take our companion by the arm as a caution against slipping. In any event, we would become alert and watchful until we had successfully negotiated the icy patch.

Like that dangerous patch of ice is the definite hour we set aside at meditation during which to be alert to temptations to our predominant fault. As we approach that hour, we can remind ourselves that this is the zero hour and, as it begins, say a prayer that we may negotiate it successfully.

Thus, although we have not been able to foresee all the circumstances of our temptations, we have been able to plan ahead definitely to some extent. At our particular examen, we have but to check our conduct during the hour of the alert. If we sincerely plan ahead like this for a definite, limited time, we can be sure that God's grace will not be wanting to remind us to pray when we are being tempted at times other than the zero hour.

❧

You must be on guard against the first signs of temptation

The second practical difficulty sometimes experienced in carrying out our resolution is this: we are faithful in resolving, but when the temptation comes, we commit the fault before we think of the resolution, the very means we chose to overcome the temptation.

The reason is that we have not developed a sensitivity to the beginnings of temptation. We have not learned to recognize spontaneously and instinctively the first signs of approaching danger and the threat of disaster. If the average motorist were accustomed to say, as we do about our faults, "I'm always involved in the accident before I recognize the danger and think of using the means to avoid it," what a carnage would besmear our highways! The motorist has developed such a habit of recognizing incipient danger that he spontaneously and instinctively reacts to it. He does not have to go through all the steps of saying to himself, "There is a car pulling out of that side street at the right. I must now release the accelerator, step on the clutch with my left foot, and apply the brake with my right foot." He does all that instinctively and spontaneously, almost without thinking, because he has developed that habit.

Why has the motorist developed that habit in the material order, while we have not developed it in the spiritual order? "The children of this world are wiser in their generation than the children of light."[22] The reason for the difference between the motorist and us was stated in the first chapter of this book: the motorist has *motivated* himself to achieve a goal; we have not.

The motorist made the civic right to drive his own car such a practical and desirable good to himself that he loved it and determined to get it. Therefore, no effort was too great a price to pay to reach that goal. He laboriously learned to drive; he practiced stopping and starting, turning and backing and parallel parking. All this he had to do in order to pass the test to get his permit to drive.

But beyond this, for other very strong motives, he wants to remain a good driver and maintain his habit of recognizing danger immediately, long before he is involved in it. He loves his life and does not want it snuffed out. He loves his shining new car and doesn't want it marred or destroyed. He loves his pocketbook and doesn't want to deplete it by paying damages

[22] Luke 16:8.

to other motorists with whom he might collide. So, lest what he loves suffer harm, he has carefully developed and preserves an alert watchfulness for the first signs of approaching danger and immediately uses the means to avoid it.

Now, this is a hard saying, yet it seems that the motorist loves his car and his money more then we love God. But, what other conclusion remains? It will be so until we motivate ourselves to love God, who has first loved us; until we motivate ourselves to love Him so much, and to fear so much to hurt Him in the least way, that we will spare no effort to develop a habit of recognizing instinctively the first beginnings of temptation to hurt Him; that we will go to any lengths to develop a habit of using immediately the means to avoid this — namely, fulfilling our resolution to pray when we are tempted.

Until that time, we shall continue to find ourselves staggering away from the shambles of one wrecked resolution after another. Until we have motivated ourselves really to *love* God, to do what He wants, instead of what we want; to want what He does, instead of what we want done, we will be still lamenting the fault before we think about our resolution.

Your examen should be forward-looking

But if that was the case with us at examen time this noon or at examen time yesterday, let us remember that the particular examen must not look only to the past. It is not a question of crying over spilled milk; it is a determination, first and foremost, not to spill the milk again! The examen should be forward-looking. We don't go to examen to weep tears for the faults we committed so much as to form a resolution not to commit the faults in the future. We trust we are sorry for sins we have committed, but the chief purpose of the examen is to resolve not to commit them this afternoon, or tonight, or tomorrow morning. Let us approach it, then, with a positive attitude. Let us approach it with a new determination to motivate ourselves never to want to hurt God again. And let our motive in this always be the motive of any Christian: not to *feel* good, but to *be* good. Let it be to do God's will.

Chapter 6

&

*Allow God to sanctify you
through the people, things,
and events in your life*

❧

God's dealing with us and God's work of sanctification in us is a twofold process. First must come the emptying of ourselves of attachment to self-will and of sin, in order that, second, we may be filled with the life of God, that God may fill us with Himself. Self-will and God's will are incompatible.[23] So, in proportion as we empty ourselves of self-will to allow God's life and grace to flow into us, we shall be sanctified.

If a child at the beach has a pail full of sand and wants to fill the pail with water, he must empty out the sand. To the extent that he takes out sand, he can replace it with water. So, too, to the extent that we empty ourselves of the sand of self-will, we can be filled with the life-giving waters of God's grace. Sometimes taking out the sand is a long and tedious process, picking out, as it were, one grain at a time with tweezers. That is so when we are taking out the sand ourselves.

But God is a partner in this emptying process. Whether we ask Him or not, He is vitally interested in our emptying of

[23] For a discussion of charity, the companion virtue to obedience in doing what God wants, see the very detailed treatment in the chapters "Love of the Poor" and "Love of Enemies" in my book *Keys to the Third Floor*.

ourselves and is constantly furnishing the means whereby this may be accomplished. The means He furnishes are the creatures and circumstances about us and the contacts we have with them. He is constantly coming to us, to work in us through the action of His creatures on us and through our contact with creatures. We seldom think of all the endurings and events to which we are subject at every moment of life as God's action on us; yet, in overlooking this fact, we miss their most significant and most valuable aspect.

∞

The Holy Spirit comes to you invisibly and visibly

Each year we prepare for the coming of the Holy Spirit into our souls at Pentecost in order that He may fill us with grace and with life. The Holy Spirit comes to us on Pentecost, as at any other time, to the extent that and in proportion as we have made room for Him; in the degree that we have emptied ourselves of self and self-will, He comes to sanctify us, because He is the Sanctifier.

But the Holy Spirit comes to us not only at Pentecost. He constantly comes to us, to act in us, to sanctify us. Otherwise we would not be sanctified. But He comes in a particular way on Pentecost because then we commemorate and relive His first coming. In view of that, we prepare ourselves in a particular way to receive Him. We prepare ourselves to let Him operate in a special way in us.

But whether on Pentecost Sunday or at any other time, the Holy Spirit comes into us in the same way as He came to the

Apostles. He comes in an invisible way, and He comes in a visible way. He came, as we know, to the Apostles in an invisible way through the infusion of sanctifying grace and a greater intensification of the divine indwelling. He came also in a visible way, through the creature *fire*, tongues of fire, suspended over the heads of the Apostles.[24]

So, too, He comes to us, first of all, in an invisible way, through the infusion of new grace and greater intensification of the divine indwelling in us. He likewise comes in a visible way, not through the creature fire, as to the Apostles, but through every other creature with whom and with which we come in contact.

⚜

Every creature is God's instrument

This is a fact that we customarily ignore. We like to think of the Holy Spirit coming to us and of God working in us in His invisible way. That is, we like to think of God's coming through the infusion of grace, through His strengthening of our soul and invigorating us, that we might be transformed and sanctified in a painless way, while we sleep, as it were, through the operation of the Holy Spirit.

But we forget about God's *visible* coming to us and His visible visitation of us through the creatures with which we come in contact. We forget that every single thing and person, animate and inanimate, that touches on or affects us in any way is God's instrument, through which He is operating in us and

[24] Cf. Acts 2:1-3.

sanctifying us, especially by giving us an opportunity to empty ourselves of self-will. If all of creation and all creatures are instruments that Almighty God has given us to grope our faltering way to Him, then, for a greater reason, *everything*, every creature, is an instrument through which God carries out His work of sanctification in us. God uses *everything* as a means to sanctify us and to bring us to Him.

That is why St. Paul tells us that to those who love God, "all things work together unto good."[25] *All things!* He excludes nothing, the good, the bad, or the indifferent. If we wish to know the extent to which all things work together unto good, we have but to recall our divine Lord's telling us, "Not a hair of your head shall perish" without His knowledge and without His permission.[26] The falling of a hair is not, certainly, an important event; and yet, even that, insignificant as it is, is a concern of God's care. So concerned is God with a falling human hair that He took the trouble, so to speak, to reveal it to mankind, to make it a part of the deposit of Faith, a part of that body of truth which God revealed to man in an extraordinary way and preserved for all eternity in the written record of His revelation. So finely does God calculate and take into consideration all things in regard to us that even the very hairs of our head, He tells us, "are numbered."[27]

Thus, He never ceases coming to us; He never ceases acting in us at every moment of our lives, not only invisibly

[25] Rom. 8:28.
[26] Luke 21:18.
[27] Matt. 10:30.

through His grace, but visibly through the action of creatures with which we come in contact and which come in contact with us.

Furthermore, in all this coming into us and in all this operating in us, God has a purpose. His purpose is that He may make us more like Him; that He may give us an opportunity to unite our will to His, thus emptying us of another grain of the sand of self-will, so that we might become more sanctified still. His purpose is that by our uniting our will to His, we may thus glorify Him, and, as a result of that, achieve a greater share of His happiness, which He wills for us for all eternity. That is God's general purpose and plan for us in all the events and circumstances of our life.

To achieve this master plan, this ultimate objective that He has for us, God directs every particular and individual event of our lives, however insignificant it might seem. God's general overall plan for us links together all the infinitesimally small events and happenings of our lives into what He now sees — and we shall one day see — as an intelligible and intelligent whole.

God sanctifies us through creatures

In every moment of our life, from the time we wake up until we go to bed at night, God is working out His plan in us. He is laying, at every instant, the particular stone that He knows is needed according to the condition of the structure of our individual life, which is demanded by His master plan in order that He may build up in us the likeness of Himself.

A Handbook of Spiritual Perfection

In somewhat the same way as a stone mason will sort over
and pick out just the right stone that has the right size, the
right shape, the right hue and color, the right texture to fit
into the pattern that he is working out in a building, so God
does with us. He is the stone mason; we are the building. He
picks out the stone that, at any given moment, may be needed
to enlighten our mind, or to strengthen our will, or to purify
our senses in order to achieve His purpose. In our judgment, it
may have the strangest kind of shape and color and texture. It
may seem the most misshapen, misfitted stone in the world for
Him to lay in the structure of our life at the particular moment; but He knows the need of it. He knows the condition of
the structure of our life, the state of our spiritual welfare. He
knows what is needed, and what must be done, and what can
be done. What must be done, He is doing at every moment of
our life, all the while yearning to complete His work, to see the
fullness of His operations in us.

So, He comes to us and He acts in us in every single one of
the events of our life in order to accomplish His purpose. But
our likeness to Him is increased in us only to the extent that
we are docile to His operation; it is decreased in us to the extent that we hinder His operation by resistance. He comes and
He works in us and operates in us, not as we think He should,
or as we would like Him to, but as He knows is best.

If our contacts with creatures affect us adversely, we call it
suffering, and here is the chief area of our resistance to God's
operation in us. But God intends even suffering to detach us
from ourselves and to attach us to Him. However, He is able
to accomplish His intended work in us through our suffering

from contact with creatures, only insofar as we submit to His operation upon us, only insofar as we are docile to His action within us by what He sends us.

If our loving Father is to achieve his purpose, we must submit to His action without reserve, without anxiety and curiosity and murmuring, like a trusting child. But so often we are like spoiled children. We pray (sincerely, we think) for God to make us holy. We ask it every day. Then God takes us at our word. He begins to work in us in the best way possible at the moment for His purpose. He starts to work in us through the contact of some creature with us. It may be a disagreeable duty; it may be a change of mission; it may be a contradiction, a provocation by someone toward whom we have an aversion; it may be a headache or other physical indisposition; it may be a regulation by a superior; it may be an interference with our plans; it may be a refusal of a permission or a misunderstanding; it may be anything that we do not like, great or small.

But at the first slight contact with the creature that is God's instrument for sanctifying us, we begin to scream and kick and yell. We say, "No! No! Not that! Don't work in me in that way! Why does this have to happen to me? What did I do to deserve this? Why do things have to be this way? Why do they have to act like that? Why does she have to do or say that?" In such manner we go on and on like pouting, immature offspring, complaining and rebelling against God's wisdom and goodness. Thus, we persist in proving the insincerity of our prayers to God that He take us into His hands to make us holy.

A Handbook of Spiritual Perfection

We are not and cannot be sincere in our desires or prayers to be perfect or to be holy unless we refuse to make peace with a habit of complaining and murmuring against God's will; unless we are willing to develop a habit of recognizing His working in us through creatures; unless we work to acquire a facility in trustfully submitting without rebellion and without resentment to the action of our loving Father on us, His children.

This submission, of course, is not to the unpleasant thing, the evil that we bear, but our submission is to the action of God that is taking place. We submit to the will of God, which is bringing about this suffering or this pain that we call evil.

Now, when we mention the will of God and evil in the same breath, we are dealing with a topic that is a scandal and a stumbling block to many, even among the so-called good and learned. Yet Catholic theology teaches that nothing happens in this world unless God expressly wills it, with the exception of sin. As St. Augustine says, "Nothing happens unless the Omnipotent One wills it to happen, either by permitting it to be or by doing it Himself."[28] God is the universal cause, the first cause of everything that happens in the world, except sin. No fate or fortune or chance or accident can either smile on us or frown on us to bring us good or to bring us bad. We read in the book of Ecclesiasticus, "Good things and evil, life and death, poverty and riches, are from God."[29] Here we have

---

[28] St. Augustine (354-430; Bishop of Hippo), *P.L.*, XL, 276; quoted in Tanquerey, *Theol. Dog.*, Vol. 2, 294.
[29] Ecclus. 11:14 (RSV = Sir. 11:14).

the inspired word of God telling us that good things as well as evil things are from God.

⤏

Some evils are evil only from
a human point of view

But how can evil be said to be from God? Before we can answer this question, we must make a distinction. There are two classes of things that we are accustomed to call evil, from our point of view. The first class is what we might term physical evils or natural evils, such as hunger, sorrow, storms, suffering that arises from earthquakes and floods and fires, illness, death, and things of this nature. They are called evil by us because we do not like them and we do not like to suffer their consequences.

But the fact is that they are not real evils in the sight of God. They are more properly called the fruits of sin and bitter medicines administered by the Divine Physician of souls. These things are evil only from our point of view. They all have positive reality and being. Therefore, they were all necessarily created by Almighty God and received their being from Him, and therefore they are good, because everything that God created is good.

Of course, from the very beginning, God's will of good pleasure was that man should not suffer. When He created man, He gave him immunity from suffering, immunity from sickness, immunity from death, immunity from ignorance and concupiscence and temptation to sin. He willed that man should not suffer these things; but He willed it *conditionally.*

97

The condition was that man not sin, that man obey His law, that man live up to his part of the agreement with God. But when man failed to observe this condition, God's will manifested itself in His willing the consequences of sin to come upon him in order to achieve His purpose in creation.

Therefore, ultimately, all suffering, all pain, all sorrow, all misunderstanding, and all disorder is traceable to sin. It is willed by God now *per accidens;* that is, God wills the natural and physical evil, but for the greater good He brings about through it. But it was not so from the beginning. His will originally was that we should be preserved from all these calamities on condition that we did His will. We did not, and hence God wills the natural consequences of sin upon us.

For example, we think of cancer as being evil. But cancer is a reality that was created by Almighty God for a purpose, and it is good. A good cancer is a cancer that does what it is supposed to do, i.e., kill somebody. We think of it as evil because it makes us or our loved ones suffer; but God made cancer to work out His Providence among men, even though, had man not sinned, He would not have willed man to suffer from cancer; He does so now only for the good of the universe. How many souls have returned to God and saved their souls because they were thus stricken? How many have become saints from the patient endurance of the sufferings of cancer? It is an instrument of God's justice, His mercy, and His love.

Again, we call a hurricane evil; but God created it, and therefore it is good. A good hurricane is one that blows things down, for that is what God made it to do; although, again, He wills it thus *per accidens* in order to bring about a greater good.

All such things are evil only from our point of view. These physical things that we call evils, evils of nature, are not evil in themselves. All of them God wills. He creates them; He brings them into being for His own good purposes. They could not exist without or apart from the will of God.

৵

God wills the effects of sin

But in addition to the physical consequences of sin that we call evil, there is a second class of evil, the only real evil, which is moral evil, or sin itself.

Now, what is the relation of sin to the will of God? Here again we must make a distinction. In every sin, we can distinguish two aspects. First of all, there is the *guilt* of sin, or the evil will or intention in the sinner. Second, there are the *effects* of that sin, or what the theologians call the *punishment of sin.*

The effects of the sin are seen in the sinner himself and in all those who suffer from his sin. For example, there are the humiliations, the discomfort, the injury that we suffer from somebody else's sin, because somebody slanders us or maligns us, or because somebody does us an injustice or an injury. Now, God does not will positively the guilt of sin in that person. That is contrary to God's goodness. But, *per accidens,* and to work out His plan in the world and thus achieve the ultimate good, God does will the *effects* of that man's sin, both on the sinner himself and on us who suffer from the man's sin. These effects of sin are not moral evil, and unless God willed them in some way, they could not happen. They are, again, physical evils, as we term it, or natural evils. So, if we set aside in our mind, or prescind from or except the actual guilt of sin in a man's will, all of the effects of sin, all of the punishments we suffer from our own sin or the sin of another are caused ultimately by God; they are willed by God; and they are pleasing to God, for they are working out His Providence in this world, which is as it is because of sin.

∞

God permits moral evil

But although God wills the punishment of sin, he only *permits* the evil will or the guilt of sin to exist. For example, suppose a man were to throw a hand grenade over the wall of a schoolyard and kill nearly a hundred children and then flee in a stolen car. All of those acts that the man did God willed, or the man could not have done them. He could not lift the grenade to pull out the firing pin with his teeth unless God gave him the strength. It is the same motion that God gives him strength to perform when he lifts food to his mouth on a fork. He could not move his legs to run to the stolen car unless God gave him the strength, for that is the same motion that God would give him to walk to church on Sunday. He could not reach out his hand to start the motor unless God gave him the strength, just as surely as a bee cannot buzz its wings unless God wills it, as truly as a mosquito cannot bite unless God wills it. Those physical actions that the man performed were not evil in themselves. It is not evil to pull a firing pin with the teeth. It is not evil to throw an object.

The evil was in the man's will, and that evil was from him and not from God. It was a lack of good that should have been in the man's will, just as darkness is a lack of light. Ever since God said, "Let there be light,"[30] the only way to produce darkness is to shut out that light. So, too, the only way to produce evil is to shut out the good that should be in the human will. So, then, we must say that God permitted the evil will of the grenade thrower, but He willed *per accidens* the effects on the children and on the schoolyard, effects that we call evil, but that really are not evil in the sight of God, because through them He works out His purposes for His honor and glory and the greater good of men.

Perhaps an example will clarify how the man's will is the cause of evil in the man's action, which God wills. Suppose we have a blister on our heel. We can walk, but we walk with a limp. It is painful; it is awkward to walk. But what is the cause of that limp? Is it our soul or life principle that gives motion to our foot and enables us to walk, and without which we could not walk? No, our soul moves the foot in the same way it did when the foot was healthy. It is the blister that causes us to limp. The blister is an obstacle that stands in the way of the motion that our soul imparts to our foot.

So, too, God is the first cause and the power behind every action that a sinner does. What is the cause of the evil in the action? The blister, that is, the man's own bad will, which interferes with God's motion and stands between it and the effect He would produce.

So, we can say that sin, the only real evil, is from God in this way: He permits the evil will or guilt in a man, but

[30] Gen. 1:3.

101

positively wills *per accidens*, as has been said, all of the effects of sin or punishment of sin. Otherwise they could not possibly exist. Therefore, we should attribute nothing to chance, or to fate, or to the ill will of men. It is wrong to say that something happened because of someone's ill will toward us. "This happened," we say, "because she hates me. This happened because she wanted to hurt me." No. God has arranged it all. God guided the hand that struck us, God moved the tongue that slandered us, and God gave strength to the feet that trampled us. They could not move unless God willed them to move. Almighty God says of Himself, through the prophet Isaiah, "I form the light and create darkness. I made peace and create evil."[31] God said, "I create evil." He creates evil by permitting the guilt of sin but positively willing the effects of sin, the suffering that comes from sin, again, *per accidens*, to bring about our greater good and His honor and glory.

But it is imperative that we know clearly and precisely what we mean when we say that God permits sin. Does saying that God permits sin mean that God sits idly by, doing nothing to prevent evil? Does it mean that He is not interested; that He looks down as an idle spectator while men assail one another, while men fight and quarrel with one another, while men hurt one another, ruin justice, and bring sorrow on one another? No, not at all! Such a conclusion shows a rank misunderstanding of the nature of God's permissive will. Furthermore, this very misunderstanding of the nature of God's permissive will causes untold discontent and unhappiness and

[31] Isa. 45:7.

misery and a lack of advancement and holiness in the spiritual life in many. In order to have a true understanding of the nature of God's permissive will, we should always remember that it must be confined to the question of real evil as such, the evil of sin, moral evil.

To repeat, the *only circumstances* in which we can speak of God's permissive will or say that He permits something is when there is a question of moral evil, or sin. *Everything else* that we are accustomed to call evil, including the effects of sin, God wills positively, even though such would not have been the case had man not sinned. So let us not be apologizing for God. He knows what He does, and He has no need of our apologies when He strikes with apparent evil either us or someone whom we are trying to comfort.

Physical or natural evils, which cause disturbance, pain, suffering, and death, such as poverty, imprisonment, disease, illness, humiliation, and so on are not evil in themselves. They are not evil from God's point of view. They are the instruments He wills to use to empty us of self-will, to correct us, and to give us a chance to merit a higher place in Heaven by carrying the cross and being more like Him. They are evil only from our point of view, just as bitter medicine is not evil from a mother's point of view but only from her child's. She knows it is a good, calculated to make her child better. The child thinks it is evil, but it is not really.

So, too, all the things for which we are accustomed to apologize for God for letting happen by saying He permits them, all these natural physical evils are not really evil. Let us, then, even if no one else will, profess faith in God's wisdom and goodness and say the truth that God *wills* them for our own greater good!

But our question now is how does God permit the evil of sin? Is it with some kind of passive permission, such as we might have when we would say, "It is snowing out, so we will let it snow because we cannot do anything about it"? Not at all.

God does not permit things because He cannot do anything about them. He does not permit things as we might be said to permit what we cannot prevent or what we would prefer not to have happen. The reason is, first, that everything that will be or that will happen in this world, even sin, God foresees. He knows about it and has known for all eternity. Furthermore everything that is, or will be, or that can happen, even sin, God could hinder, God could stop if He so wanted. But since He does not stop or hinder either sin in general, or any particular sin, He must be said to want it or will it in some way. Thus, from all eternity, Almighty God decreed and willed to permit sin. Therefore, God permits sin, not by being unwilling that it happen, but by willing to permit it. There is in Almighty God a positive will of permitting the evil of the guilt of sin.

God can draw good out of evil

Why God permits the evil of the guilt of sin must remain ultimately one of the great mysteries of our life. St. Augustine summed up all the possible reasons for it by saying that He permits the evil or guilt of sin in order that He might draw out of it a greater good than if He had not permitted the sin. This is true even if we cannot see the greater good that He brings about. Sometimes we can, but our ability or inability to see the greater good alters not one iota the fact that God does produce greater good from the sin He permits than would be if He did not permit it.

For example, God willed to *permit* the sin of the murder of His own divine Son. But He did not permit, but *willed* the nails to go into His hands and feet, the thorns to pierce His brow, and the spear to pierce His side. Those effects of sin He willed; the guilt of the sin, the evil will in the men's heart, He permitted. And that permission of sin which Almighty God willed redounded to the good of the whole human race. It showed forth the goodness and the power and the majesty and the love of Almighty God. If God, from all eternity, had not willed to permit that sin of deicide, we would not be able to kneel today in the presence of the Most Blessed Sacrament. We would not be able to read His doctrine in these pages.

Actually, God's drawing good out of evil shows the wonders of His Providence. Anyone can produce good from good, but it is a sign of greatness to draw good from evil. For example, any licensed pilot should be expected to bring in, in good weather, a plane that is in sound condition; but it is a mark of a great pilot to bring in a plane in a raging storm when all the engines but one are out and the landing gear is broken. So God's drawing good out of evil is a sign or mark of His power and greatness.

Hence, by the wickedness that He permits in some men, He stimulates others to goodness and virtue and sanctity. For example, God willed to permit the evil of guilt in Hitler and so many inhuman Nazis and communists who ran the concentration camps during World War II. God willed to *permit* their evil will, but, *per accidens*, He *willed positively* all the suffering and the misery borne by the prisoners in those camps. Because of that suffering, many of them are saints before the throne of God today, singing, "Holy, holy, holy, Lord God of hosts,"[32] who would not be there had God not permitted the evil will and the sin of their persecutors. But whether we in any way can see what good results might come about, we know that the cause in God for His permitting the evil of the guilt of sin is that He might draw greater good from it.

Therefore, if we complain about what happens to us from the sin of others, we are complaining about what God wills for our greater good. This complaining marks the difference between the saints and us. They saw God as the doer of everything that happened to them. They disregarded altogether the evil will and sin of the one who offended and injured them and concentrated only on the thought of the effects in them. Consequently, they saw God's will as the primary actual and efficient cause of everything that happened to them. They were secure in the knowledge that God is so good that He would will and could will nothing to happen to them unless it was for their own greater good.

Those who injure us do God's will

Thus, those who hurt or injure us by sin act out a dual role: the first part is that in which they have an evil will, in which

[32] Cf. Isa. 6:3.

they devise an evil plan against us; the second part they play is
that in which they have power to and are able to externalize
their evil plan, to put it into action. In this role, they play the
part of instruments of God. They are doing God's work, even
though they may be ignorant of it, because, in reality, God is
willing for us the effects of those sins. Through those effects,
God is working in us to empty us of self, that He might fill us
with His grace and His will, that He might give us an opportunity to merit a higher place in Heaven by bearing the cross as
He did.

Thus, we see the folly of complaining about what happens
to us, because to do so is to complain against the merciful hand
of God. St. Augustine points it out in this way: If we find fault
with those who by sin and by bad intention hurt or injure us,
what are we really finding fault with? Are we finding fault with
their evil will? Or are we finding fault with their power and
ability to put that evil will into action, so that we suffer the effects? Or are we finding fault with both? It is useless, he tells us,
to find fault with their evil will, because if they only have an
evil will against us and are powerless to implement it or to put
it into action, they can never hurt us. They are like a roaring
lion in a cage; it cannot get out, so it cannot hurt us. We can
stick out our tongue at it with impunity. So, too, others' evil
will cannot hurt us unless they have power to externalize it,
that is, to say that word or to do that thing against us which
their evil will is ordering.

But we must not complain about their power to put their
evil will into effect, because that power they get from God. It
is God working in them. Thus, when we complain about the

power they have to perpetrate their evil, we are complaining about God. As St. Paul says, there is no power but from God. Any tongue, any hands, any lips, any mind that injures us receives the power to move and to injure us from God. Thus, if it came from God, it is praiseworthy.

Again, we must recall here that God can permit or will nothing that is not for our greater good. God does nothing unjust against us or against anyone. If one man kills another, God permits the guilt of that sin and cooperates in giving the power to do it. True, the man kills the other man unjustly, but God does not permit the sin unjustly. So also, the unjust will of the murderer is to be condemned, but the just permission of God is to be praised, as God is to be praised in all of His works.

⚜

Work to overcome your feelings
in your sufferings

So, it will be a happy day for us when we are able to rise above merely natural feelings of suffering and sorrow in trials, and perceive and realize God's working within us by means of present suffering. The more insensible we become to natural human feelings of suffering and pain, the more we will overlook them, the more we will become alive to the astounding fact that Almighty God, our Father, is stooping, as it were, at this very instant, to work out His plan in our own soul through this thing that is happening to us. The more we are willing to forget self in our trials, the more we will recognize that *Digitus Dei est hic* ("the finger of God is here") right in our very own life.

Allow God to sanctify you

Of course, we shall continue to *feel* these sufferings. No amount of virtue will ever deprive a man of his sense of feeling. But, we shall not dread affliction that comes upon us. Adversity will befall us, it is true, but it will not overcome us, because we shall know that it is God's will for us, that it pleases God that we have this adversity, and we must struggle to ensure that it please us, too.

So, the more we are able to rise above our feelings in our trials, the more we shall be aware that God is stooping to be interested in us, to sanctify us, to bring us to a greater capacity to glorify Him and enjoy His happiness by means of all these events that transpire in our life. If we could only see that and recognize that, how fortunate we would be.

But we know from bitter experience that it is difficult to accept sufferings well. Often a slight trouble can cast us down, and a slightly greater trouble can crush us. We are such tender, hothouse flowers that we dread and cringe from every touch of the wind, of the rain, of the sun, of the frost. Our habit of seeking self-satisfaction, of seeking our own pleasures, our own ease, seeking to satisfy our aesthetic tastes and so on, has made us soft, incapable of putting up with anything that is difficult.

Because we resist God's purifying action of suffering so much that His work in us does not bring about the progress that He intends it to bring. Instead, it seems to increase our guilt or our imperfection. We become embittered and impatient with suffering, and we revolt against it. If we do submit, too often it is with murmuring and complaint. But in showing ill will and resentment toward suffering, we are repulsing God and His loving operations in us. We are obstructing the fatherly operations by which He wants to sanctify us.

Therein lies the tragedy of living by our senses; the tragedy of judging everything by our feelings, by our comfort, our ease, our pleasure, our freedom from pain. Therein lies the tragedy of living merely natural lives according to the maxims of the world. We misjudge the love of God acting in us, and we repel and insult His love, for it is an insult to murmur against the operations of God's love in us.

How often have we frustrated, literally frustrated, God's efforts to sanctify us? How often have we repelled Him in the past — just when His love was sending us, in its most austere but most merciful disguise, the thing that we needed most! For all suffering, no matter how it comes, is God coming to us, God operating in us. Every suffering that comes to us from contact with creatures has a mission to perform in our soul for God. This mission is to purify us of self-will, to uplift us, to free us from ourselves. It is sent by God, and it is our duty to accept it.

When we recall, for example, that St. Vincent de Paul would never have a fire in his room in order that he might accept the cold as God sent it, when we recall that St. Benedict Labre[33] would permit insects to sting him without brushing them aside, we begin to have a dim view of the tremendous scope there is for the pure and simple acceptance of daily sufferings through which Almighty God comes to purify and sanctify us.

---

[33] St. Benedict Labre (1748-1783), pilgrim and mendicant saint.

Allow God to sanctify you

Strive to see how creatures work to sanctify you

So, whether the day is Pentecost or any other day, God the Sanctifier comes to us. He comes to us as He came on Pentecost, invisibly, by His grace. He also comes visibly to us through the instrumentality of the creatures with which we come in contact at every single moment. Our contacts with these creatures will produce sanctification in our souls according to our reaction to and our attitude toward them.

We are sanctified only when we see and embrace and cling to God and His will in every single person and thing and circumstance and event in our life. In embracing them, remember that it is His will, and it is His action in us that we must love and embrace, not the evil thing, not the disagreeable thing itself. We must embrace His will with our will and our mind. Nothing must be allowed to separate us from His will.

Like St. Paul, we must be able to say, "I am sure that neither death, nor life, nor angels, nor principalities, nor things present, nor things to come, nor powers, nor height, nor depth nor any other creature will be able to separate us from the love of God, which is in Christ Jesus, our Lord."[34] "I am *sure,*" he said. He could say this because he had weighed every one of them, things present and things to come, height and depth, and so on. He had measured them all with a single eye, the eye of faith, and he saw them all as instruments by which God sanctified him. Therefore, he was sure that, having recognized them as instruments, he could never be separated from God by them.

[34] Rom. 8:38-39.

To see that fact, to recognize the hand of God in every person we meet and every event that happens to us, to realize Him in every circumstance of our life is the sum of all the gifts of the Holy Spirit that God could give us, because this is one of the greatest truths in the world that we could know: God is constantly operating in us through the circumstances of our lives, to sanctify us, by emptying us of self-will in order that we may be filled with Him.

That is how He sanctified St. Paul and all the saints; that is how He will sanctify us, by coming to us and operating in us through the instrumentality of all the creatures with which we come in contact. If we have been resisting His sanctifying action, let us begin now to develop the opposite habit.

Chapter 7

♣

*Abandon yourself
to God's will concerning
your spiritual state*

❧

When we are thinking of the things we would like to do in the spiritual order — the faults we would like to overcome and the virtues we would like to acquire — it is beneficial for us to ask, "*Why* would I like to do these things?"

In liking to do these things, is God really in our plan? Is His will in our considerations at all? There can be many motives for our wanting to do all those things that we "would like to do," many motives for our wanting to acquire certain virtues or overcome particular faults. We could want to do so because we would feel good about it; we would be able to taste the sweet fruits of success in the spiritual combat. Or, we would like to overcome these faults so that we could look good, so that never again would we be embarrassed by having someone see us fall into them; or never again would we be humiliated by being admonished or corrected for the particular fault that weighs us down.

Again, we might want to do all these things so that we could measure up to the ideal that we have of ourselves. We might like to overcome these faults so that we would not have to struggle against them anymore, so that we would not have to worry further about reproaching ourselves for these failures.

A Handbook of Spiritual Perfection

Our motive might be to have a kind of peace of mind by being able to look God in the face without having our failure loom up between us.

Again, we might want to be rid of these faults and acquire this particular degree of perfection so that we might reach a plateau where, we hope, we could rest in peace. Once there, we would have this desired virtue automatically; we would not have to worry about striving to practice it. It would be, we think subconsciously, somewhat like a writer learning to type by typing the material he composes. It is easy to imagine his wishing to get rid of the faults that he has in typing, so that when typing becomes a confirmed habit — when he does not have to give it much thought — he can then give all of his thought and effort to his creative writing.

So it is possible to want to be rid of our faults and to acquire virtue so that, having done it, we can rest and be freer to devote our attention to other things. We would then have more time for our duty, or be able to have more concern for our work or hobbies.

All these are possible motives for wanting to do "all the things we would like to do." All of these could be motives for wanting to overcome faults or acquire virtues.

But none of them is a true supernatural motive. None of these motives is truly a motive of faith or of love of God, because all the motives mentioned for overcoming our faults leave God out of the picture or have God only vaguely connected with the goal.

We make a mistake in viewing our own perfection as an objective to be sought apart, somehow, from God — as separate from God — as if our perfection had objective reality independent of God, which, of course, it does not have, nor will it ever have.

Because we fail to see our perfection as being achieved only when we are being absorbed in God, because God is only vaguely connected with our true goal, therefore God's help in achieving that goal is forgotten, is not thought of, is not adverted to. And when God's help is not thought of or adverted to, when it is not constantly in our minds, the inevitable result follows. The task seems too great for us because we depend on ourselves.

In such a situation, we are like St. Peter walking on the water. Confident, a victim of indiscrete zeal, trusting in himself, he started to climb out of the boat and walk on the water toward our Savior. Our divine Lord let him fall into the inevitable result of self-trust, which is faintheartedness and discouragement. Peter began to be afraid of the wind and the waves; he began to sink. Only when he forgot his self-confidence and his trust in himself and his own efforts, and turned to Christ humbly and trustfully, only then was he saved.[35]

So, like Peter, we confidently plan all the things that we would like to do, all the faults that we would like to overcome and the virtues that we would like to acquire. In our self-confidence, we decide we are literally going to run on our way to sanctity. But we no sooner have one foot over the gunwale of the boat when we find ourselves beginning to sink. Then we quickly become discouraged.

[35] Cf. Matt. 14:28-31.

As with St. Peter, so in our case, the only answer to the problem is to confide in God and avoid trusting in ourselves and our own efforts. We must develop absolute confidence in the infinite wisdom and power and goodness of God. He is infinitely wise, and He knows what is best for us; He is infinitely good, and He wants what is best for us; He is infinitely powerful, and He can do and will do what is best for us.

Therefore, the only answer to our difficulty in this problem of our growth in perfection, as in all problems, is to conform to the will of God. For the perfection that we seek and the perfection that God wants for us is nothing other than the union of our will with His will. It consists only in wanting at every moment what God wants.

Perfection is wanting what is

We prepare best and most perfectly for union with God in the moment to come by accepting completely and absolutely every one of the circumstances of this precise moment now. That very attitude, having our minds and wills united with God, is, in itself, perfection. It is in itself union. Without it, there can be no perfection. There cannot be even the seeking of perfection if our wills are not united with God's will. This union of our will with God's will must extend even to the condition of our soul, even to the degree of perfection we have reached at any given moment, because all of those circumstances are God's will.

"But suppose I am in sin; suppose I feel miserable?" Well, we should thank God, then, for the way we feel. For the way we feel is part of the circumstances of the moment. That circumstance and all other circumstances in the world, from the buzzing of a mosquito's wings to the length of the stride of an ant on the sidewalk, are God's will. Therefore, they are the best things that can be at that moment. They reflect God's glory, and they work unto good for those who love God, who wants things that way at that moment and has arranged them so. So, in exact proportion to the extent that we want what God wants, including our own spiritual state at this precise moment, our next moment will be better. So, also, we will be better, because perfection and holiness are synonymous with union of our will with God's will.

⚘

You may still desire holiness

"But," we say, "suppose I really want to be a saint; suppose I desire perfection. Shouldn't I be unbearable to myself as I am? Shouldn't things be different from what they are now? How can I be satisfied with what I am now if I want to be a saint?" Well, the answer to that question is both yes and no.

In your desires for holiness, yes! Go as far as you want; go as far as you can. Desire the very stars! Desire to be holy, and let your desires carry you into eternity, into the very arms of God Himself! In desire, covet as much holiness as you possibly can. In effort, also, put forth as much as you can! Strive for holiness as much as you are able; strive as if everything depended on you, and pray as if everything depended on God.

But in our will, here and now, we must want what *is* — now! We must want what is now, because that is what God wants, and that is what God has arranged; otherwise it could not be that way. So, no matter what our desires for holiness might be at any moment, we *are*, in fact, what God has willed us to be.

If now, at 4:15, we are what we are, it is God's will.

Thank God for it. *Desire* to be a canonizable saint at five o'clock; *work* with all you have to become a canonizable saint by five o'clock. You may be worse by then than you are now; you may be better. But whatever you are, thank God for it, because that is what He wills; that is what He wants. It is His will; otherwise it could not be that way. But no matter what we are at five o'clock, desire, by six o'clock, to be a saint all over again. If by six o'clock, you are much nearer sanctity, thank God for that; if not, thank Him also, for that is His will.

Our footsteps along the road to perfection, of course, are bound to lag behind our desires. It cannot help being that way. For example, if we are to make a trip to our home in New York from Baltimore, we are foolish not to desire to reach there; we are foolish if we are not there already in our mind, wishing we were there and thinking of when we shall be there. But the reality is we are still in Baltimore, or near Baltimore, and all the fretting and worrying about it in the world won't get us home to New York any faster. It will only distract our attention from the essential business of travel. It will hinder our getting there as fast as we otherwise would if we were not worrying.

Progress requires conformity to God's will

Conditions are the same on the road to sanctity, on the way to Heaven, on the way to holiness. If our desires did not run ahead of our actual steps, we would never reach our goal. But remember this: we *are* on a journey, and we cannot get there overnight; it is a lifetime's journey. Each day we should thank God for the progress we have made up to that point. However much we may strain in desire and want to be at the goal, each day we make only the mileage that God would have us make. Today, perhaps, we made only five miles. Tomorrow we might *want* to advance ten miles, but actually we accomplish only two because of the snow of self-will or bad habit. So, independent of our aspirations, wherever we are at any given moment of our journey, we are at the point God wants us to be, plan as we will otherwise. For our progress is according to God's will and God's plan, and not according to our own.

We, on our part, must cooperate with God's will and with all His inspirations. We must be led by the Spirit of God. As St. Paul tells us, "Whoever are led by the Spirit of God, they are the sons of God."[36] We must be docile to His directions at every note. That is all any of the saints ever did. A saint never wants to advance one step faster or further than God wills; he never wants even to put his foot into Heaven before God's sweet Providence would have it so, for the saints lived only in accord with God's Providence and His will.

Perfection necessarily implies our *wanting* to make the progress that God would have us make; but this necessarily means we must conform our will to the progress that we have made at any given moment of our lives.

[36] Rom. 8:14.

That very conformity is a major part of the progress that God wants us to make. All contrary thoughts are merely manifestations of the impatience of our own will to have God hasten our journey to holiness according to our own ideas, instead of according to His plan. This, note well, is one of Satan's most subtle temptations, with which he tries to delude those who are striving to be holy and who are really seeking perfection.

As long as he can keep them stirred up and unconformed to God's will, at least in the matter of their spiritual state at any given moment, to that extent Satan has disunited them from God's will; to that extent they have failed to reach the perfection that God would have them reach, because perfection consists in uniting our will with God's will in everything, including our degree of perfection, even though we with our puny minds cannot see the wisdom of what God wills.

So, what God wants of us is to want what *is*. In particular, He wants us to want what is in regard to our spiritual state, because whatever that is, is God's will, unless we are in sin. Even in that event, the guilt of that sin is His permissive will from which He intends to draw greater good by our repentance. Those who want everything, every single thing, every single circumstance, every single action, above all, everything about their spiritual state exactly as it is now, at this moment, because God has arranged it so — they are the saints.

⌘

You may wonder, "Why try?"

But an answer must be given now to an objection that might occur to many: "Because God has willed that I be what I am now, and holiness consists in my wanting that, does it mean that I must want to stay the way I am now?" God forbid! As has been said, it merely means that God wants me to be what I am now, and therefore I must thank Him for it. But that is *this now*. I do not know yet what He wants me to be in the *next now*. In the next now, He may want me to be something completely different. I know with certainty that He wants me to try to be something better in the next now, for He has said, "Be holy because I am holy."[37] Again, He said, "Be ye perfect as your heavenly Father is perfect."[38] Again, "This is the will of God, your sanctification."[39]

But, the objection continues, if we will be what God wants us to be at any given moment, what is the use of our trying to be more perfect? Such a question is reminiscent of the Pilgrim who was starting out through the woods without his gun. His wife remonstrated at his temerity, pointing out that he might be killed by Indians. He answered that if God willed him to be killed, he would be killed whether he had his gun or not. His wife replied, "But suppose God wills you to be killed on condition that you don't have your gun with you." In her wisdom, she knew that God wills some things absolutely and other things He wills conditionally. The condition, in many instances, is something that depends on us, such as our prayers or our acting in a certain way. Thus, we must try to be perfect because that is God's will for us. We know with certainty that

[37] Lev. 11:44.
[38] Cf. Matt. 5:48.
[39] 1 Thess. 4:3.

unless we try to be perfect, we cannot be united with His will at all.

Therefore, this doctrine is in no wise a case of fatalism or quietism. Catholic teaching is that whatever is, whatever has happened, is God's will, with the sole exception of the guilt of sin, which is His permissive will. Otherwise, whatever is could not have happened, for God is the universal cause of all things, except for the guilt of sin. But it is also true that no perfection is possible for us without our doing God's will. And His will is that we strive each moment to be better.

Consequently, thanking God for what we are now does not mean that we want to stay what we are now. It does not, above all, mean that we can stay such with impunity. We must *want* to be better in the next now, and we must *work* to be better. God will give us the grace to be better, to be completely different. We must strive to cooperate with that grace as much as we can. But, an hour from now, we must again rejoice in what we are at that now. And so on to the following now, and the succeeding now; always, at every now, our will must be completely united with the will of God for all time and for eternity.

Therefore, as has been said, things cannot be different from what they are at any given now, or moment, because they are the way that God has arranged them. To want what God wants, particularly for ourselves, is to fulfill the counsel to cast our cares upon the Lord.[40]

To want what we are now, and to strive to be a saint in the next moment; and as the next now comes along, to want what

[40] Cf. 1 Pet. 5:7.

is at that new now, but strive to be better in the following now — what is that but finding Heaven right here on earth? For what is Heaven? Heaven is where there is no past and no future, but only the present — an endless, eternal, infinite succession of nows, in which our will will be completely united with the will of God.

Chapter 8

*Learn to
make your confessions
more fruitful*

A question that must occur to all periodically is this: "Why am I not better?" When we think of all of the aids we have in living our spiritual life, it would seem that we should make more rapid progress. Consider one of these aids: the sacrament of Penance, which we have at our disposal week after week and which should contribute to our constant spiritual improvement. Very often, we find it does not produce that result. We might ask ourselves why this is so.

Perhaps a clue to the answer might be found in the parable our divine Lord told about the sower going out to sow his seed. Some fell by the wayside, some on stony ground, some on thorns, and so on. But He said, "Some fell upon good ground and brought forth fruit, some a hundredfold, some sixtyfold, and some thirtyfold."[41]

Now, note that all the latter was good ground, and yet it brought forth varying degrees of fruit. So, too, our souls are essentially good ground for the reception of the sacrament of Penance; we have the essential dispositions to receive the sacrament validly and licitly. And yet, because of defects of our

[41] Cf. Matt. 13:8.

disposition, we do not receive the hundredfold of fruit that we might receive and that our Lord wants us to receive from our confession.

So, then, importance must be attached to the answer to the question "How can I derive more profit from my confessions?" First, we must be clear on the purpose of the sacrament of Penance in relation to God's plan for us and our holiness.

God's plan for our sanctification consists essentially in His raising us to the supernatural state of adopted sonship by uniting us to the Mystical Body of His Son. From our union with the Mystical Body, we participate in and live with the life of God called *sanctifying grace*. We are likewise assured of the actual graces necessary to live the supernatural life. As a consequence, we have the power, in every moment of earthly life, to glorify God on earth and to increase our supernatural capacity to glorify Him forever in Heaven and consequently to enjoy His happiness forever there. The only thing that can interfere with God's plan for us, and consequently the only real evil in the world, is sin. Mortal sin completely destroys God's plan for us, and venial sin interferes with its perfect accomplishment.

But God in His goodness was not content to let us run the risk of losing His incomparable gift of supernatural life forever, through our own foolishness, by mortal sin. To prevent this, He devised a second plank of salvation — as the Fathers of the Church called it — a means of sanctification and salvation having a twofold end. It would be the means by which, if we had the misfortune of losing the supernatural life by mortal sin, we could regain it; and it would also be the means whereby we could, while still retaining it, grow and increase in the supernatural life. That means is the sacrament of Penance.

Our divine Savior in His goodness instituted Penance to be a means of peace for souls troubled by failure in their efforts to love and serve Him. Consequently, anyone who foolishly makes the sacrament of Penance anything but a sacrament of peace is using it contrary to the intentions and purposes of our divine Savior. When we approach Confession, we do not go before a prosecuting attorney. It is the only court in the world in which the defendant is his own accuser.

Above all, we should remember that in this sacrament, we appear before a kind and loving and merciful Judge who is willing and eager to forgive us. Each time we go to Confession, we offer God an opportunity to exercise His greatest prerogative which, St. Thomas tells us, is His mercy, an attribute even greater, in a certain sense, than His justice.

In considering the sacrament of Penance from a practical point of view, and with the purpose of making its frequent reception a more productive factor for good in our spiritual life, it is convenient to divide it into three distinct parts, or three different actions on the part of the penitent.

Examine your conscience

The first act of the penitent is the preparation for Confession called the *examination of conscience*. Before beginning this examination, we should ask Almighty God to give us a knowledge of our sins and a hatred of them such as He has. We should beg Him to give us the grace to see sin — and especially our own sins — as He sees it.

This cannot be done, of course, in a few minutes after rushing to church from some absorbing occupation when it is time for Confession. We cannot, it is true, always choose the time we would like to go to Confession, but we should make our preparation for Confession at some time we do have available, even if it is the night before. But no matter when we do it, it certainly seems that fifteen minutes is not too much time to devote to preparation for such an important sacrament as Penance. In fact, one of the saints used to say there were two things we should be ready for at any moment: death and Confession.

While we are examining our conscience, two extremes are to be avoided: one is to be slipshod, and the other is to be scrupulous. A good rule of thumb is never to use more than half the time of preparation for Confession in examining our conscience. Generally, if we go to Confession frequently, about five minutes is sufficient to examine our conscience.

In the process of examining our conscience, having prayed to the Holy Spirit for light, we should look first of all for mortal sins. This, of course, is not generally a statewide manhunt for which we have to organize a posse. If, God forbid, there are any mortal sins on our soul, they are not hidden away in a corner under the dust. They are prominent in red and blue neon. Moreover, they are flashing on and off in our attention. We know they are there without having to look for them.

But if, please God, there are no mortal sins, we look for the venial sins we have committed since our last confession. We

Learn to make your confessions more fruitful

look particularly for deliberate venial sins and, more particularly, for deliberate venial sins against the greatest of the virtues and, consequently, the gravest of venial sins in themselves — namely, venial sins against charity. We look for venial sins against charity in speech, in thought, and in action. Then we look for deliberate sins against the duties of our state in life, particularly those against obedience and abandonment as we saw in the chapter on our predominant fault.

In searching for these venial sins, we should look for the ones that are the most serious, the ones that stand most in the way of our progress. It is not necessary, of course, in examining our conscience, to go over every thought we have had since our last confession, every person we have spoken to, every place we went, and everything we did, trying to think up an interminable list of peccadillos and sins and failings.

There are those who make the examination of conscience a *"tour de force"* of their memory, a sheer exhibition of the ability of the human mind to recall everything they might have done since their last confession. They may arrange their sins in logical order, or in numerical order, or in some original order of their own conceiving. When, at the end of examination time, the memorization is complete, they come in breathless to the confessional and sputter their list like a Fourth of July sparkler burning out. Their memory feat endures just about as long as the ephemeral sparkler. Once it has sputtered out, it is gone, nevermore to be rekindled. But the worry about it is not gone. Leaving the confessional, such penitents begin to wonder whether they told all their sins, how many they forgot, and whether they were all understood just as they were in reality.

All such straining is, of course, completely foreign to and a travesty of the wonderful memorial of the mercy of God that is the sacrament of Penance. God is not interested in multiple computations. The faculty that must operate to obtain pardon is not our memory but our will. God forgives us our sins, not because we remember them well, but because we are sorry for them in our will.

Be sorry for your sins

Hence, after examining our conscience, the major portion of the preparation time for Confession should be devoted to the most important part of our confession: being sorry for our sins.

There are circumstances in which our sins can be forgiven without our examining our conscience. For example, if we were struck unconscious by a car, a priest could give us absolution and forgive our sins, even though we did not examine our conscience at all. As a matter of fact, we could not do so, because we would be unconscious.

Again, there are circumstances in which our sins can be forgiven without our confessing them. Soldiers going into battle cannot possibly have time to go to Confession. Yet, the chaplain can give them absolution *in globo*, as it is called, and their sins are forgiven, if they are sorry for them and intend to confess them when they have an opportunity. Or, to refer again to our previous case, if we are unconscious, we cannot confess our sins, but still they can be forgiven.

So, there are circumstances in which sins can be forgiven without our examining our conscience or even confessing our

Learn to make your confessions more fruitful

sins. But there are no circumstances under God's blue heaven in which our sins can be forgiven without our being sorry for them. Here we have touched the very heart of the sacrament of Penance, the most important part — namely, *contrition.* We must be sorry for our sins if we are to have them forgiven.

But please note well precisely what has been said: we must *be* sorry; not, we must *feel* sorry. These are two vastly different acts.

Feeling sorry is in the emotions, in the feelings. We could feel more sorry about seeing a cute little puppy run over and hurt in the street than about the gravest confession we ever made. That is, we could feel greater sorrow in the sensible order, manifested by the shedding of tears and other signs. That would be *feeling* sorry; but that is not what God asks of us in regard to sin. We must *be* sorry; and being sorry is not in the emotions but in the will. Being sorry for our sins means that we hate the sin we have committed and have a firm determination not to commit sin again. The essence of sorrow is the regret or hatred of the evil we have done, accompanied by the firm determination, with God's help, of not committing it again.

Obviously, the sincerity of our sorrow, when we come out of Confession, is found by asking ourselves what we have resolved not to do again. Suppose a companion were to walk up to us and slap us in the face and say, "I am sorry. I didn't mean it." But, if at the time of the apology, we knew that the next time we met coming around the corner, that companion intended to slap us again, we would not think much of the sorrow. So, too, when we kneel down and tell our Lord that we are sorry for having slapped Him in the face, that we are sorry for having hurt Him, if He can read in our hearts that the next time we face the same occasion, we will not resist any harder than we did in the past, He does not think much of our sorrow.

Father Nash, S.J., somewhere in his writings gives an example to show the futility of such sorrow. Following his thought, let us picture Christ, after His scourging, sitting in the court-yard of Pilate, the drunken rabble and the soldiers mocking Him. See Him there, clothed in an old purple rag with a crown of thorns on His head, a reed scepter in His hand. See the drunken soldiers with their mailed fists coming up and slapping Him, then genuflecting and spitting at Him and railing at Him, between swigs out of a bottle. Poor, gentle Christ!

Then imagine one soldier stepping forward from that crowd, reeling toward Christ. Suddenly a hush comes over them all. They fall back afraid, wondering. They watch breathlessly as they see that big, burly soldier go up and kneel before the gentle Christ with an apparent change of heart. They hear him say, "Master, I am sorry for my part in this. I am truly sorry." Then, when the hush has completely subdued the crowd, imagine him standing up, wiping his mouth with the back of his hand and then hauling off and striking Christ across the face again, laughing jeeringly and getting the others to join in the laugh at his mock sorrow.

Just the relation of such an incident strikes horror into our hearts. Yet is that not precisely what we do when we go to Confession to tell our Lord we are sorry and at the same time have no intention of ever doing anything about that antipathy, about that unkindness, about that uncharitable speech, about that impatience, about that bitterness? We tell Him we are sorry, we pretend that we are sorry, but in reality we have no intention in the world of doing anything to change; for all practical purposes, we intend continuing to do the same thing over again.

Yet, unless we are sorry for our sins and intend, with God's help, to do what we can to avoid them in the future, they are not and cannot be forgiven. Thus it is possible to confess venial sins and not have them forgiven, because we are not sorry for them.

We can be sorry and be as fearful as we will that we might fall in the future; but the purpose of amendment means that here and now, our intention and our resolution is, with God's help, to do everything possible to try not to commit this sin again. We will use all the means necessary not to fall into this deliberate sin again.

It is not difficult to stir up such sorrow in our hearts and wills if we only think of the motives that we have for being sorry. If anyone in the world had done as much for us as our Lord has, and we continued to treat him with the same coldness and contempt and indifference that we show our Lord, we would not have a friend in the world. We would not be able to look ourselves in the face with any respect. In a word, the crucifix, the Passion of Christ, is the greatest motive in the world to stir up true sorrow for our sins.

Since being sorry for our sins is the most important part of our confessions, we should spend the greater part of our time of preparation for Confession in stirring up this sorrow. The act of contrition, the act of sorrow that we make during the

A Handbook of Spiritual Perfection

actual administration of the sacrament of Penance is merely
an external sign to the confessor that we are sorry. The only
way he has of judging our sorrow is by that act of contrition.
He has to take our word that we mean it. But if we wait to get
into the confessional before we try to arouse our sorrow, the
distractions of listening to the absolution or thinking about
what penance the priest has given us, and so on, make poor circumstances in which to stir up true sorrow for our sins. Hence
the wisdom of being sorry before we enter the confessional, for
it is the most important part of Penance. Hence the importance of asking Almighty God for the grace of sorrow while as-
sisting at Mass on the morning of the day we go to Confession.

The true sorrow we arouse for our sins at examination time
does not, of course, militate in any way against our thanking
God for the fact that we are not much worse than we are, that
we do not have worse things to confess than we have. It recognizes that God's grace and God's goodness alone have pre-
vented us from falling even lower. If we are troubled and upset
at seeing ourselves down, that upset is not from love of God; it
is from love of self. If we really knew ourselves as we are, if we
were truly humble, instead of being surprised at seeing ourselves down, we would wonder how we were ever erect.

❧

Confess your sins

The third act of the penitent after the examination of conscience and the stirring up of contrition for our sins is the actual telling of our sins to the priest. In this, all God asks is that
we be sincere, that we accuse ourselves as we know ourselves

138

Learn to make your confessions more fruitful

to be before Him. This can be done without difficulty if we exercise our faith and recall to whom we are confessing our sins.
We are confessing our sins to God, to our divine Lord, through
His representative, the priest. We are confessing our sins to
Christ, who already knows them better than we do. He knows
in what we are guilty. He knows our weakness, He knows our
heart, and He knows our record. We cannot deceive Him. It is
so much easier to confess our sins if we keep in mind that we
are speaking to our divine Lord Himself, who already knows
our hearts and what we have done and who has decreed that
we humble ourselves by telling our sins to Him through the
ears of one of His ministers.

It helps, further, to remember that the priest, the representative of our Lord to whom we confess, no matter whose confession he hears, knows that there, but for the grace of God,
goes he. He is a human being like his penitents. And he has
the grace of office by which, once he walks out of the confessional, he can ignore whatever he has heard. The good Lord
knows he has problems enough of his own without carrying
ours around with him.

Furthermore, after his study of theology and human nature,
and his years of experience in dealing with sinful humanity, after what he knows of his own heart and his own weakness, if
we think that a Johnny- or Jenny-come-lately like us is going
to disclose a new kind of sin that will literally knock him off
his chair, we are very foolish. Yet, that is the way the Devil can
work on us at times. So very often he takes away people's
shame when he induces them to commit sin, then gives it back
to them when it is time to confess it. Succumbing to that

139

shame, they conceal its cause in confession, and thus they make a very sad and tragic mistake.

❧

Try to find and confess the cause of your sins
In the confession of our venial sins, so often we say, for instance, "I was disobedient." That is what we did, but do we ever tell *why* we were disobedient? It could be for many reasons: because we were proud; because we were arrogant; because we were moved habitually by human respect. Again, we might say, "I was uncharitable." That is what we *did*, but what we *are* is self-opinionated, attached to our own judgment, intolerant of any opposition.

When we are confessing our venial sins thus, when we take the trouble to try to discover and to mention the cause, the root fault that underlies the surface rash, we produce a twofold beneficial effect. First, we realize more vividly our sins and their intrinsic nature and evil and are thus more strongly motivated to avoid routine in confessing them and to struggle more courageously against them. By confessing the underlying causes of our external faults, we likewise invite direction from the confessor, who, seeing that we care enough about our own advancement to use some means to achieve it, is moved to interest himself and apply his efforts to the same end.

❧

Know what you should confess
Having treated of the manner of making a confession, the question remains: What *should* we confess? But even anterior

Learn to make your confessions more fruitful

to that, we should know what we *must* confess. That is, what do we have an obligation to confess? For our peace of mind, it should be recalled that all we *have* to confess, all that there is an obligation to confess, is the number and kinds of mortal sins that we are certain we have committed.

Any youngster in catechism class knows that for a mortal sin there must be grievous matter, sufficient reflection, and full consent of the will. We must be dealing with some act or omission gravely sinful; we must know what we are doing and do it despite its sinfulness. That is a mortal sin. Sins of that kind are all that we have an obligation to confess. Other kinds of sins we do not have to confess. We may; it is often good to; but we do not have to.

Here, incidentally, a word of caution is in order. When it is said that mortal sin requires grievous matter, sufficient reflection or knowledge, and full consent of the will, the knowledge in question must be had at the time we commit the sin to matter. Suppose that five years ago we committed a sin, and at that time we did not know the act was sinful, or, at least, we did not think it was mortally sinful. Now, five years later we learn that what we did five years ago was, in fact, a mortal sin. Sometimes we conclude, "My, I did that, maybe several times, and I never told it in Confession. Therefore, I have been making bad confessions all these years." Then begins the big worry! But such worry is useless and wrong.

It is wrong for this reason: any subsequent knowledge we acquire about an act that we did in the past does not change at all what we thought about it at the past time, nor any guilt that was then incurred. If we did something yesterday and we did not think it was a mortal sin, but tomorrow we learn it was mortal, still, for us that particular act was not a mortal sin at the time we did it. On the other hand, if we did this something yesterday and we thought it was a mortal sin, but tomorrow we learn that it is not a mortal sin, then, for us it was a mortal sin at the time we did it. This is so because we are judged according to what we do with what we know. Hence, as we learn more and more about the spiritual life and the virtues, let us not foolishly stampede into worry and concern because of new things we learn about things we did in the past. God judges us only on what we do with what we know.

While on the subject of doubt, it is good to recall that doubtful sins are not matter for absolution. If we do not know whether we consented to such-and-such a sin, then, for us it is not a sin. We may, for peace of mind, confess such as a doubtful sin. For example, we can say, "I do not know whether I gave in to this, or whether I was fully voluntary in doing this, but I would like to confess it as it is before God." We may do that, but we should never confess doubtful sin as certain, or by the same token, certain sin as doubtful.

Returning to the question of what we should confess, it is clear that all we have to confess are the number and kinds of mortal sins. But if, please God, we have no mortal sins to confess and want to receive sacramental absolution and the grace of the sacrament, we have to confess at least one venial sin. The reason is that the sacrament of Penance is a judgment made on sin and cannot, therefore, take place unless a sin is confessed. But, no doubt, every one of us, if we search our hearts and our reins sufficiently deep, can find at least one venial sin that can be matter for absolution and reception for the graces of the sacrament. The venial sin we confess can be of our present or past life, either already forgiven or not.

St. Vincent de Paul advises us never to confess more than two venial sins or three at the most. The reason is the difficulty of having specific sorrow for, and making resolutions about, and being determined to avoid even that many in the future. Thus, he tells us to concentrate on two or three. It would be most difficult to have firm resolutions of amendment about long enumerations of venial sins, week after week. Furthermore, any venial sins for which we are truly sorry are forgiven in Confession, even if we do not confess them.

Thus, among those two or three venial sins told in Confession, we should mention those about which we took resolutions in our last confession.

Above all and before all, we should confess the sins of our predominant failing, on which we are working for our practice. As mentioned in the chapter on the particular examen, we should make that sin part of the matter of our confession, in fact the focal point of it. Whether it be ambition, or pride, or sensitiveness, or whatever it might be, we should confess that sin each week along with its causes, trying to cut down the number of times, the number of occasions on which we fall into it. If last week we confessed that we fell eight times, we should resolve that, with the help of God, next week it will be down to four. When next week comes, we might have to say seven or even nine times. No matter! At Confession, we tell God we are sorry and take a new resolution for the following week. The grace of the absolution will strengthen our resolution and give us additional help to keep it for the succeeding week.

At the end of Confession, we should always mention some sin of our past life. The reason is that we will thus be sure to have sufficient matter for confession. Secondarily, but also importantly, it is an act of humiliation. That it may be truly salutary from the penitential viewpoint, we should pick out some sin of our past life that we might be ashamed or embarrassed or humiliated to tell. Such confession is a good act of penance in itself, and the sacrament of Penance the best place to do penance.

 ❧

Offer thanksgiving after Confession

After we have left the confessional, we should never let it be said of us what our divine Savior was forced to say of the ten lepers: "Were not the ten made clean? . . . Has no one been found to return and give glory to God except this foreigner?"[42] When our divine Lord absolves us of our sins in the confessional, He does something far more wonderful than He did when He cleansed the lepers of their leprosy. That was merely a physical disease, whereas in Confession something supernatural takes place: the forgiving of sins — a greater thing, says St. Augustine, than the creation of the world.

Our thanksgiving will consist, first of all, in devoutly fulfilling our penance. We must never forget that the simple little penance that the priest gives us has a value in reparation far

[42] Luke 17:17-18.

Learn to make your confessions more fruitful

exceeding what it would have if we merely chose it as a penance ourselves. When we fulfill the penance imposed upon us
by the priest in Confession, the merits of the Passion and
death of Christ accompany it and plead with the Father for the
remission of the temporal punishment due to our sins.

After we have done our penance (if it can be done at the
time), continuing our thanksgiving, our minds will be occupied with thoughts of the goodness of God and of our desire
not to sin again and our determination to die to sin. For example, suppose we had deliberately offended, in a cantankerous
moment, someone we love very much. Later, we repented of it
and went to ask pardon, to say how sorry we were. Suppose she
received us most graciously, told us to forget about it, that she
would never think of it again, that she did not want us to think
of it again, and that things were just as they always were between us. As we arose and left her presence, what do we suppose our thoughts would be? We would be thinking of what a
wonderful person she was, how good and how kind and how
Christlike, and of how miserable we felt for having hurt her
and offended her, and how we were going to make it our business to see that we never did such a thing again.

When we sin, we offend Almighty God, who loves us more
than anyone in the world can possibly love us. We offend Him
whom we want to love. Therefore, when He has forgiven us in
Confession, when He has told us to forget about it, not to
think of it again, if we have any sensitivity, any love for Him at
all, our thoughts will follow the same vein. We will think of
His goodness to us; we will think of trying to make it up to
Him, trying to see that we do not offend Him like that again.

We will think of ways in which we can pay the debt of temporal punishment that still remains to be paid even after He has forgiven our sins.

As the saintly Abbot Marmion suggests, what better way to pay this debt of temporal punishment than to offer, through the sacrament of Penance we have just received, all of our acts of mortification and renunciation and penance of the coming week in order that we may die more and more to sin? In this way, we make the fruits of our confession extend throughout the whole week. We increase the value of those acts of penance. We say to our divine Lord, "Dear Jesus, I offer You all the acts of mortification, of renunciation and penance that I am going to do this week, whether voluntary or imposed by others. I offer them all to You to make it up to You for the sins You have just forgiven me and to pay part of my debt for the temporal punishment due to my sins, which will one day hinder and delay my seeing You." Isn't it wonderful that God in His goodness will accept those pitiful little acts of penance that we do, will accept our offering of them to pay our debt of temporal punishment due to our sins?

Let faith make your confessions more fruitful

As with so many other spiritual problems, the answer to increasing the fruits of our confessions is to arouse our faith in what happens there. The Curé of Ars[43] summed it up by saying

---

[43] The Curé of Ars (1786-1859), St. John Vianney, patron saint of parish priests.

Learn to make your confessions more fruitful

that when we go to Confession, we should be mindful that we are about to take Christ down from the Cross. We are about to take the nails out of His hands and His feet, to lower Him gently in our arms, remove the crown of thorns from His head and rest it on our breast to try to comfort Him. When we go to Confession, we are making God happy, because we are giving Him an opportunity to exercise His greatest attribute: His mercy.

Every time we go to Confession, even if we confess only venial sins, the Precious Blood of Jesus is offered again to the Father for our individual pardon and our individual forgiveness. Every time God absolves us through the lips of His priest in Confession, it is as though all of the suffering and all of the merits, all of the Blood of Christ, all of the love of Christ were offered again to His heavenly Father and applied to our individual soul. To stir up our faith in that fact at Confession not only pleases God mightily, but also prevents anything like routine from creeping into our confession.

Every time we go to Confession, we should strive to put ourselves in the disposition we would want to have if it were the last confession we were to make; we should strive to make it as we would want to make it were God to call us immediately after the sacrament or before we had a chance to go again.

If we do this, we shall walk into the confessional each time conscious that our divine Lord Himself, at that moment, is offering to His Father again the last drop of His Precious Blood, all the merits of His Passion and death for us and for the remission of our sins. We shall be conscious that the Most Blessed

Trinity is occupied with us at that moment, as if we were the only soul in the world. We shall be aware that as Christ is forgiving us, so also the Father forgives us and is about to send the Holy Spirit into our souls with new graces and that, consequently, God Himself is about to dwell in us with new intensity. This is the glory and the splendor that can be our confessions!

Chapter 9

Seek to please God in all you do

❧

"Whatever you do, work at it from the heart, as for the Lord and not for men, knowing that from the Lord you will receive the inheritance as your reward."[44] The purity of intention that St. Paul here recommends to us, which determines the value and merit of our actions and the extent of our reward, can be described very simply as having one aim, one intention, and one motive in everything we do: to please God. Purity of intention is the manifestation of the virtue of simplicity.

Our divine Lord has said, "If thy eye be sound, thy whole body will be full of light. But if thy eye be evil, thy whole body will be full of darkness."[45] The figure our Lord uses here is rather strange sounding to our ears. However, by *eye* He means the intention of an action, and by *body* He means the action itself. Therefore, if the intention of an action is good, the action, He says, will be good; and if the intention for which we do an action is bad, the action itself will be bad.

But there are degrees of purity of intention. Our intention is purer the less there is of self and self-will in our reason or motive

[44] Col. 3:23.
[45] Matt. 6:22-23.

for doing things. The purer our intention is, the more meritorious our actions are and the more glory do they give to God.

A Christian lives, or should live, for that very purpose. That is the primary reason for which all creation was made: to give glory to God. God made us for Himself, that we might glorify Him and, consequently, that we might participate in His happiness. St. Paul tells us, "Whether you eat or drink, or do anything else, do all for the glory of God."[46] If we do that, we merit the peace that surpasses understanding,[47] the peace that God decrees and gives as a result of living as we were meant to live and fulfilling the purpose of our existence, that peace which is the tranquility of proper order.

Peace, then, is the result of striving to please God and not other people or ourselves. By working with purity of intention, we give glory to God and bring happiness to the angels and the saints and our divine Lord in Heaven. "There will be joy in Heaven," our Lord said, "over one sinner who repents."[48] But that doesn't mean that the angels have to wait for sinners to do penance before they can have any joy. The angels and saints share in the joy of God when He is glorified by His creatures.

Purity of intention can bring even worldly success
Actually, working to please God, working for a pure intention, working not for ourselves but for the sake of God, results

[46] 1 Cor. 10:31.
[47] Cf. Phil. 4:7.
[48] Cf. Luke 15:7.

very often, not only in peace, but even in worldly or material success. Wrong motives, on the other hand, seem at times to have a way of vitiating our powers and efforts. As St. Thomas à Becket[49] is made to say in the play *Murder in the Cathedral*, "The last temptation is the greatest treason — to do the right thing for the wrong reason." Purifying our intention can often spell the difference between worldly success and failure.

Bearing cogent testimony to this thesis is a famous basketball player who had been an outstanding star not only in prep school but throughout his college career. However, during his senior year, his performance began to fall off badly. He would shoot and miss one basket after another. Everyone asked what the matter was with him, but no one seemed to know, least of all, he himself.

One day he was talking with one of the priests on the faculty at his university, trying to get at the root of his trouble. The priest questioned him about every conceivable factor, every possible angle of his problem. They tried to discover any circumstances existing at the time of his slump that were not existing previously.

Finally, the priest, in his probing, put his finger on something that seemed significant. In recent months, the basketball player had been keeping steady company with a girlfriend. At recent games, she had been sitting in the crowd in Madison Square Garden. He admitted, at last, to the priest and to himself, that every time he got his hands on the ball, he was

---

[49] St. Thomas à Becket (1118-1170), Archbishop of Canterbury and martyr.

thinking of his girlfriend up in the stands; he was putting on a show for her benefit, trying to make a basket to please her. Consequently, he was tense; he was pressing, trying too hard; he was not his old self.

The good priest recommended as a remedy that he try to purify his intention in playing basketball. Let his aim be to give glory to God through the use of his athletic talents and abilities rather than vainly to show off. "But, Father," he said, "in the midst of the bedlam in Madison Square Garden at a big basketball game, how can I have time to purify my intention, or how can I think to keep it pure?"

After much discussion of the point, they agreed that he would try this: every time he got his hands on the ball and was going to shoot for the basket, just as he would let the ball go, he would say, "For Thee!" That was all. It would take only an instant. "For Thee!" That would be enough to purify his motive and to tell God that he was shooting that basket for Him and for His honor and glory.

Subsequent games proved that to be the remedy which enabled him to overcome his motive of pride, for which he was working before and which was destroying his basketball finesse. To achieve such worldly success, of course, is a poor motive for which to strive for purity of intention, but it does show how, if we are working to please God alone, we do not strain inordinately for results. Consequently, we achieve better results than if we were pressing or tense as a result of trusting in ourselves instead of in God.

However, the essential effect of purity of intention, or working to please God, in addition to glorifying Him and meriting for ourselves, is the peace that God intends us to have. It is that peace which results from right order, which comes from fulfilling the purpose of our existence by doing what we do to please and glorify God.

Learn how to tell whether your intention is pure
We might ask whether there are any ways by which we can know whether we have purity of intention. After all, it is very easy to deceive ourselves in this matter. We can say we are doing what we do for God, but are we really? Is there any way we can tell for sure? Are there any signs by which we can confidently know that we're doing what we do to please God?

Actually, there are, and very infallible signs, too. We can tell whether we are working to please God alone by our attitude toward what we do, toward the results that we achieve, toward the success of others, and toward the rewards or approval that we might get or not get from what we do.

* *Our attitude toward what we do.* First, our purity of intention can be gauged by our attitude toward what we do or what we are given to do. If we have purity of intention, if we are doing what we do to please God and not ourselves, then, obviously, we are indifferent to, and, in the final analysis, will have no preference for this work or that work or the other work that Almighty God gives us to do. We are content whether He gives us this duty or that duty or the other duty. We want only to be sure that God wants us to do this particular thing, and

A Handbook of Spiritual Perfection

we can know that infallibly if it is part of the duties of our state in life or if we have been assigned to it by superiors. Knowing that our task is God's will, we are deeply glad to do it with all our heart and strength. If we ask, "Why must I do that?" we are far from simplicity and purity of intention.

Again, if our intention is pure, we put the very same effort into a fatiguing duty as we would into an easy duty; we put the same effort and enthusiasm and attention into an obscure, hidden, unglamorous duty as we would into an honorable duty, or one that would bring us praise and put us in the spotlight and cause admiration on the part of others. If we had purity of intention, our enthusiasm for any work would not be measured by personal pleasure or personal satisfaction or reward.

While He was on this earth, our divine Lord said, "My food is to do the will of Him who sent me."[50] He has made here a very significant choice of words. Food keeps us alive. We have to have food three times a day to be able to maintain ourselves. And what food is to our body, the will of the Father was to the Son. His food was to do the will of the Father. That should be our food also, no matter what position or duty we have.

The only important information we need is this: Is what we are about to do God's will? If it is, and we are doing it to please Him, it does not make any difference whether it is sweeping a floor, or giving a speech, or

[50] John 4:34.

teaching a class. If we have purity of intention, we shall put the same effort and enthusiasm into each of them and glorify God as the angels do who veil their faces with their wings and sing, "Holy, holy, holy!"[51]

If we go about the obscure, or the hard, or the unromantic, or unwanted tasks with reluctance, like a slave beaten to the burden, we can be sure we are not working to please God; we are working to please ourselves. We can know this from the fact that, since we do not happen to be pleased in this instance, we are not working particularly hard or with much enthusiasm. We are trying to get it done as quickly as we can, or leave as much of it undone as we can.

So, there we have a test: How can we tell whether we are working to please ourselves or to please God? By our attitude toward what we don't like to do.

• *Our attitude toward results.* Another test of purity of intention is our attitude toward the results we achieve in what we do. If we are working to please God, we are not upset if what we are doing does not turn out well. That is true whether we are sewing something, or polishing a floor, or sweeping, or teaching a class. If we have purity of intention, we are willing to accept God's will, even in failure. If we get all upset when what we do does not turn out well, recall that God is not upset. If we are working to please Him, why are we upset?

[51] Isa. 6:3.

Thank God that He does not judge us by results. He looks only at the effort we make with the knowledge we have, that is, the intention and motive we have in our mind and will. Are we so foolish as to think that God is dependent on our puny efforts to achieve any success? Anything that we could do in a million years, God could do in an instant, in a million other and better ways. All He wants is our loving service, the efforts of our heart and soul to please Him. If we give Him that, there is no failure possible, as long as we are doing His will, no matter what the material results of our work may be.

That is what we must be assured of. All God wants is our effort and our pure intention. "If thy eye be evil, thy whole body will be full of darkness." If our intention is wrong, then no matter what success we achieve, it is nothing in the eyes of God. On the other hand, no matter how a work may appear to fail, if we have done it with the right intention, to please God, then it is a success.

There is no possible worldly success, no potential material success that can give honor and glory to God like the service of our will, like doing His will to please Him. Did ever any work seem more a dismal failure than the work of Redemption? God's own Son came to earth, and, after thirty years of preparation, He walked the highways and byways of the Holy Land, curing and healing and teaching the people, giving of Himself night and day, praying for them, doing penance for them. At the end of three years, rejected by all but a few who could be counted on the fingers of one hand, He died spiked to a post like a common criminal, between two other criminals. Did ever anything look more like a failure than that? Yet, at the end of it, He could cry out, in a voice of triumph — the cry, not of a failure, but of a success: "It is finished!"[52] What is finished? "The work Thou hast given me to do."[53] That is success! However much it might have looked like failure in the eyes of the world, it was the greatest success ever achieved or ever to be achieved.

So it is with our puny efforts and with the works that we have to do. It is not how we succeed that matters, but how we try to do what God wants us to do to please Him. It is not how much we do of what we want to do that counts with God, but how well we try to do what He wants us to do. So, then, we know we have purity of intention if we are concerned only with doing as best we can whatever God gives us to do, leaving the results to Him, whether they be success or failure. If we have purity of intention, we accept all with equanimity, with a peaceful mind, knowing that God is glorified not by what we do, but by our intentions and the efforts with which we do what He gives us to do.

On the other hand, if we get all upset when things do not turn out well, when things we do turn out not so

[52] Cf. John 19:30.
[53] John 17:4.

glowingly, it is because our motive, our intention, was to achieve personal success. Then, when we do not, we are disappointed and sad. That is a sure indication that our intention was not pure, that we were not working for God.

Thus, we can tell if we are working for God with a pure intention by our attitude toward the results that we achieve in our work, by our attitude toward failure and success. If the thing that we do turns out successfully, we should thank God for it and give the glory to Him. "Do not rejoice in this," said our Lord when the Apostles came back boasting that they were able to cast out devils. He had given them that power, and they went out and tried it and it worked, and they came back saying excitedly, "We were casting out devils!" He responded, "Do not rejoice in this . . . but rejoice . . . that your names are written in Heaven."[54] That is the only thing in which to rejoice, not in the puny worldly successes that we might achieve, the tiny, futile, material honors we might amass. Do not rejoice in these, but that your name is written in Heaven.

In the same way, we should rejoice with God if what we do turns out unsuccessful. If we have done it for Him, He has been glorified. It matters not that we are not glorified for our lack of success. "He must increase, but I must decrease."[55]

[54] Luke 10:20.
[55] John 3:30.

• *Our attitude toward others' success.* Another test of our purity of intention, or manifestation of it, is our ability to rejoice at the success of others without being jealous of them, without being envious of them. If we have in mind only the good pleasure of God, we shall be glad at their success in their studies, in their work, in their apparent success in the practice of virtue and the overcoming of their faults.

On the other hand, if we are uneasy about their success, if we feel envious of it, if we wish they were not so successful, that is a sign that we are not seeking the glory of God; it is a sign that we have in mind, subconsciously at least, to come out on top, and that we are working for our own glory instead of God's. Because they seem to be threatening our position, we are uneasy about it, or we are jealous of it, or we are envious of their success.

If we have purity of intention, we will react as Moses did to others' success. Someone came to him complaining that another was prophesying, and Moses said, "Oh, that all the people might prophesy!"[56] In effect he was saying, "Would that God would give it to everyone to glorify Him by prophesying as He has given me to be able to glorify Him." So, too, if we have purity of intention, if we are working to please God, we shall be glad when He is glorified by anybody, even by those we like the least.

[56] Num. 11:29.

♦ *Our attitude toward the reward.* It is clear that we can test our purity of intention in these ways: by our attitude toward what we have to do, whether it is to our liking or not; by our attitude toward the results we achieve, whether they are successful or not; and by our attitude toward others' success. Finally, we can test the purity of our intention by our attitude toward the reward or thanks we receive for what we do.

If we are working to please God and not ourselves, we are indifferent to praise or blame on the part of men. If, after doing a piece of work, we are sad or upset because we do not get others' notice, because they do not praise us for it, or because they do not tell us how wonderful we are, that is a sign that we were not working for God, but for the reward or for that notice. We can tell this is so, for why else are we sad when we haven't received it?

If we are working for God, if we truly have purity of intention, we do what God wants us to do in the best way we can, even if nobody sees it, even if nobody says a word about it. After all, why should others thank us for doing our duty when we are not working for them? We are working for God, and He does not have a habit of stepping down to earth physically every once in a while and patting us on the back and saying, "That's wonderful work. Keep it up!" But while He does not do that tangibly, we do know that He is grateful. We know this by faith, and that same faith should motivate us to be pure in our intention of working to please God alone.

The same purity of intention makes us indifferent to that diabolical evil, human respect, by which we so often do what we do so that people will think well of us; or we avoid what we should do because people will think ill of us. If we act only to please God, we will destroy this demon of human respect.

✧

Purity of intention does not depend on feelings

Our sole aim, then, should be to please God in our studies, in our spiritual exercises, in our duties, in our serving, in whatever it may be that we do. "Do all for the glory and honor of God." But mark this well: inevitably there must be times when we won't *feel* like being indifferent to what we have to do, or the results that we achieve, or the reward, whether praise or blame. But feelings, let it be repeated, have nothing to do with holiness. They have no morality. Actually, the less we feel like doing what we have to do, the more merit there will be in doing it, the more will it show our love for God. For doing something when we do not feel like it shows we are not doing it to please ourselves, and thus we can be sure we are doing it for God, if we have made that intention.

The surest means to acquire such purity of intention and, actually, the test of our purity of intention, is to say, "Thanks, God," in distasteful situations. To thank God and ask Him for His helping grace when we don't like what we have to do, or when we don't like the way we are asked to do it, or when we don't like the results we achieve, to grit our teeth and say,

A Handbook of Spiritual Perfection

"Thanks, God. This is for You," and do it — that is purity of intention in action!

At such times, we are like our Lord in the Garden. He hated so what He had to do that He prayed that He would not have to do it: "Father, if Thou wilt, remove this chalice from me; but yet not my will, but Thine be done."[57] He was saying in effect, "Thanks, God. This is what You want; I will do it." So, in imitation of Him, we should strive to develop the habit of saying, "Thanks, God," when we have to do something that we don't like. Let us pray thus: "There is no satisfaction in this for me, but I will do it for You, dear God."

But our aim should be higher yet. We should strive not only to begin with that intention, but also renew it as often as we can during our actions. We should renew it especially as often as we are tempted to rebel in the midst of doing something we don't like; just as often as we are tempted to resent the results that we achieve, or be upset at our failure; just as often as we are tempted to feel sad because we do not get praise. To thank God when we do not succeed, to thank God for what we don't like, is the surest sign that we are working to please Him and that we have purity of intention. Having that, we have an added consolation: if we can thank God in the midst of things we don't like to do, thus showing that we have purity of intention, we can be sure that we shall also have purity of intention and be working to please Him in the things we like to do.

[57] Matt. 26:39, 44.

Chapter 10

✿

Be humble

＊

Humility is one of the two virtues that our divine Lord asked us specifically and expressly to learn of Him. "Learn from me," he said, "for I am meek and humble of heart."[58] Humility was the unifying principle of the whole life of our divine Lord, and it is one of the foundation stones of our spiritual life. Hence the importance of having clear notions of this virtue.

Many difficulties arise in the practice of humility because of false concepts of the true nature of humility. Very often the virtue of humility is thought of as certain external acts that *seem* humble or that we hope will be interpreted by others as being humble. In the popular mind, it signifies a kind of "Uriah Heep," hand-wringing self-depreciation, which could not possibly be meant by anyone in his right mind.

St. Bernard[59] tells us that there are three kinds of humble people, and two of them are not humble. First, there are those who *feel* humble; they feel lowdown. Perhaps they are victims of an inferiority complex. They are like the man who said that he felt so low he could reach up and touch bottom. But St.

[58] Matt. 11:29.
[59] St. Bernard (1090-1153), Abbot of Clairvaux.

A Handbook of Spiritual Perfection

Bernard tells us that because we feel low or feel humble doesn't mean that we are humble.

Second, there are those who *think* they are humble. They like to think speculatively about how humble they are and how unworthy they are. They exaggerate their own faults so others will get the impression that such insignificant failures could not possibly be real faults, and hence, their exaggeration must be due to humility. But St. Bernard says that because they think speculatively that they are humble doesn't mean that they are humble; they only think they are.

The true virtue of humility is not a matter of external acts. It is essentially an internal habit of the soul that inclines us to act in a certain way. It is a virtue that disposes us to realize our true position before God and to act in accord with that reality.

Humility is a volitional virtue that moderates our desire for excellence. Sometimes it is said that humility is truth, but more properly speaking, it perfects our *will* and has to do not so much with knowing the truth as with loving and seeking the good. However, it is based on the truth of what we really are in God's sight.

And what is our position in the sight of God?

Actually, God made us out of nothing. We are absolutely nothing of ourselves. We had nothing to do with our coming into being; we can have nothing to do with our going out of existence. True, we can commit suicide and thus have something to do with going out of this worldly existence; but our true existence is eternal and is lived either in Heaven or Hell. We are absolutely and completely dependent on Almighty God, not only for our existence, but for every single thing that

168

is needed for or flows from that existence; for everything that we have, every gift, every talent, every ability, the very breath we breathe, we are dependent on Him. We can do nothing of ourselves. "What hast thou that thou hast not received?" asks St. Paul. "And if thou hast received it, why dost thou boast as if thou hadst not received it?"[60] "Without me you can do nothing," says our divine Lord.[61]

Humility is the truth of what we are before God

But this complete helplessness and insufficiency does not present the entire true picture of us. There is more. In addition to depending absolutely on Almighty God for every gift we have, including the major gift of existence, we have abused and misused His gifts and become worthy of punishment. Therefore, not only are we not accountable for anything good that we have; but we have, by sin, forfeited our right to anything good we have. By sin we have merited any evil that could possibly befall us as a punishment of sin.

What is our true position before God? Perhaps an example will help us realize it. A television program called *Candid Camera* used to conceal motion-picture cameras and take movies of people unknown to them. Later, amid great consternation, the secret would be revealed to them. Recalling that example is a good device for helping us realize what we are truly before God and what we are in our own conscience.

[60] 1 Cor. 4:7.
[61] John 15:5.

A Handbook of Spiritual Perfection

Imagine that a candid motion-picture camera had been secretly training on us at every moment of our lives since the very dawn of reason. Suppose that, unknown to us, a complete motion-picture film of our life had been made by that camera. Following us like our shadow, it had been grinding away each moment of our life, every morning, noon, and night, every hour, every minute of our childhood and youth and until now. Then imagine that our movie was going to be shown to all our companions, our own life story, complete, as it really was night and day, alone, with others. The audiovisual record on that film is what we are before God. That is our true position before God. Humility means that we shape our conduct according to that truth.

Therefore, humility is the disposition of will to restrain the tendency in all of us to claim esteem beyond that which is our due. If we are humble, there will be no posing, no pretense, no attempts to appear better than we really are, to be something that we really are not. Humility implies all that and more!

The reason we can be humiliated is that we have not developed the habit of acting according to the rule of humility. Suppose, for example, we fell flat on our face in front of a crowd. We can imagine our embarrassment and humiliation. Why are we humiliated in such a situation? The reason is we are not humble; it is because we feel we are in a position that is somehow beneath our dignity. We are thus humiliated because we like to put on a show; we like to put up a front; we like to appear brighter, smarter, more alert than we are. We like to present a revised and expurgated version of that life movie of ours for the general public. The one that is known only to God and us must be safely hidden and guarded in the storage vaults or archives of our own conscience, because we must never appear as we truly are! Such a conviction, such an attitude, is the antithesis of humility.

Christ is the perfect model of humility

Above all, if we are acting in accord with the truth of our true position before God, if we are humble, we submit to God's will for us, particularly when that will is unpleasant or untoward. We graciously accept criticism, unkindnesses, injustices, and all the other hardships we have to bear from others. It was in this that our divine Savior most clearly manifested His humility, which He proposed to us as a model.

But to understand the unbelievable extent of the humility of our divine Lord, we must go in spirit back far beyond His public life, to the Incarnation, to the very moment of the Annunciation, for there is where His humility began to appear.

To get some faint idea of the completeness with which God emptied Himself, as St. Paul tells us He did, we would have to resort to an outlandish comparison. Yet this comparison is not so inconceivable that God Himself did not seize upon the very same metaphor to describe His humiliation in the Passion. Through the lips of His psalmist, He said of Himself, "I am a worm and no man."[62]

With that prophecy as a cue, we can imagine a fabulous situation in which a man, for some good, justifiable reason would

---

[62] Ps. 21:7 (RSV = Ps. 22:6).

be able to and would want to become a worm — actually a worm — for the sake of worms and for some good he could do for them. While still retaining his human nature, that is, his intellect and will, he would take on himself the form of a worm and be confined in his movements to the ground. He would submit to the condition of a worm and be driven up out of the ground in a sudden rain, lest he drown; suffering all the indignities to which worms are subject: being threaded on a fish hook, being eaten by robins, and so on. Such a lowering of himself by a human being is unthinkable, even if it were possible to some man.

Yet the difference between a man's nature and the nature of a worm, while tremendous, is still measurable; but the difference between Almighty God, the Eternal Creator, and the nature of man that He made out of nothing, is *infinite*. His taking on the nature of man is infinitely more degrading, if you will, than would be a man's taking on the nature of a worm. St. Paul tells of it in the only way he could say it: "He *emptied* Himself, taking the nature of a slave and being made like unto men. And appearing in the form of man, he humbled Himself, becoming obedient to death, even to the death on a Cross."[63]

To continue the fantastic analogy, we would think that even if a man were inconceivably to take upon himself the form of a worm for some reason, he would at least select a place for Himself among the better class of worms, if there be such a thing. We would think he would choose to be a ruler of some kind. We would think that if he took upon himself the nature

[63] Phil. 2:7-8.

of a worm, he would be in some position of esteem or influence. Yet, when Christ became a man, He was born in an obscure corner of the world of the obscure laboring class. He was no prince; He was no ruler. Born of humble parents, He was put to death at the end like a criminal.

Now, if we could realize that fact, we would have some notion of how God really humbled Himself in becoming man in the first place. While still remaining God, with His infinite knowledge, power, and goodness, He confined Himself to man's way of acting, thinking, walking, and so on. All the time that He was on earth, perfectly and infinitely holy in Himself, He chose deliberately for Himself all the consequences of life that He would have deserved as punishment had He been the worst of sinners like us. Of His own will, He took upon Himself all the punishments due to sin.

This was the proof and the manifestation of the humility of Christ; not His humble condition or the poverty of His life. A person can be in a lowly position and be poor without being humble at all. The humility of Christ was the internal disposition of His will to accept all the contradiction and suffering that He would have deserved had He been a sinner in truth, as we are. He submitted uncomplainingly to all the trials and tribulations and crosses of this life that flow from the malice of sin. That was His humility of action.

Humility calls you to accept all that befalls you
But we are actual sinners. Every one of us has sinned personally. And because we have sinned, we deserve to suffer in

punishment thereof. Therefore, our humility will manifest itself in the disposition of will to accept what we have to suffer in this life as justly due to us because of our true position of sinners before God. If we rebel at the "slings and arrows of outrageous fortune,"[64] if we complain about contradictions, misunderstandings, corrections, adversities, troubles, sicknesses, trials, and problems, it is because we are not humble. It is because we are not regulating our conduct in accord with that true picture of ourselves as we are before God.

If we ever committed one tiny sin, the least venial sin, no punishment on earth can fully make amends for it. God revealed this to St. Catherine.[65] To offend the infinite God, who has made us out of nothing for Himself, who sustains us in being with no desserts or rights of our own, is to reach up and bite the hand that holds us over the abyss of nothingness; it is to commit the worst kind of treason. If we have done that but once, nothing we can suffer on this earth can adequately atone for it. We deserve more than we can ever suffer in this life, either in intensity or in duration.

But so often we rebel at what we have to suffer from others. How different is our conduct from the example of the divine Lord, who resented nothing — crosses, trials, contradictions, denials, slights, ingratitude, persecution, suffering, even a cruel death. He did not use His divine power to escape one bit of it, to alleviate it one iota. He was humble! He accepted all in our stead; He accepted the Cross as we should accept it; He

[64] William Shakespeare, *Hamlet*, Act 3, scene 1.
[65] St. Catherine of Siena (1347-1380), Dominican tertiary.

accepted and suffered all that He suffered as if He were deserving of it all, as we in fact and in truth are.

The necessity of living in the midst of opposition, contradiction, trial, and suffering is a consequence of sin — Original
Sin and our own. Being humble means accepting all these
things without bitterness, without resentment, without complaint, without impatience. It means we bow gracefully to
them because we deserve much more. It means we accept all
crosses with patience.

When we are impatient, we are rebelling against the will of
God; we are resenting what God sends us; we are telling God
that He has no right to give us this punishment because we
do not deserve it. The truth is, of course, we deserve infinitely
more. Thus, if we are humble, we recognize that we merit any
suffering that comes to us, and that nothing we can suffer on
this earth can ever fully repair the damage we have done or the
offense that we have given to God by our deliberate sin.

❧

Humility allows you to see all
that God has given you

But, in addition to accepting as our just due whatever evil
might befall us, there is a positive aspect to this virtue, the
practice of which is often overlooked or misunderstood. Humility is based on truth, but the truth on which it is based is
one. Therefore, real and valid humility must be based on or
flow from the whole truth. And the whole truth about anyone
is that God has given him undeniable gifts and endowments
and talents, both of nature and of grace.

A Handbook of Spiritual Perfection

Humility, then, does not mean self-depreciation. Being humble does not mean that we must deny the endowments of nature or grace that Almighty God has given us. If God has given someone a magnificent voice, it is not humble for her to pretend that she sings like a frog or to deny in any way the gift that God has given her. Humility is based on truth, and the truth is that God has given her a truly beautiful voice. Therefore, she should not deny it, but attribute it to God, which is positive humility.

Our divine Lord Himself — infinite perfection — said to His followers: "Learn from me, for I am meek and humble of heart." But He also said to His enemies, "Which of you can convict me of sin?"[66] Thereby He proclaimed His unique sinlessness.

Our Blessed Mother did not deny the wonderful prerogatives Almighty God had lavished on her. "Because He who is mighty has done great things for me," she sang, "all generations shall call me blessed."[67] Is this the Virgin most humble? "All generations shall call me blessed." Surely, that future, perpetual benediction was a gift that Almighty God had given her, "because He has regarded the lowliness of his handmaid."[68] But note what she says: "He who is mighty has done great things for me." She claimed no applause for her greatness; instead, she put the credit for her gifts where it belonged — namely, with God.

[66] John 8:46.
[67] Cf. Luke 1:48-49.
[68] Luke 1:48.

St. Paul calls himself "the least of the apostles."[69] That is what he was of himself. But he also says, "But, by the grace of God, I am what I am, and His grace in me has not been fruitless — in fact I have labored more than any of them."[70] St. Paul was saying in effect, "I have labored more abundantly than Peter, the first Pope, the one whom Christ made the head of His Church; more abundantly than James and John, who went up on the mountain with Him; more abundantly than Philip and all the others. I, Paul, have labored more abundantly than all of them." Talk about boasting! No! Not at all, for he explains, "Yet not I, but the grace of God with me."[71] He gave the credit where credit was due.

Similarly, St. Thomas Aquinas claimed to have the gift of never reading anything that he did not understand completely and remember always, but he did not attribute this gift to himself; he attributed it to God, where it belonged.

The difference between our Blessed Mother, St. Paul, St. Thomas, and all humble ones, and ourselves is that they attribute their gifts and prerogatives to their proper source, which is Almighty God, our Father.

On the other hand, we so often childishly attribute our gifts and accomplishments to ourselves. "See my medals? Am I not grand?" How foolish can we become? We are like a man driving an armored express truck, transferring gold and securities from one bank to another. Wouldn't he be foolish to drive

---

[69] 1 Cor. 15:9.
[70] 1 Cor. 15:10.
[71] Ibid.

by his girlfriend's house and pretend that all the gold in his truck was his own? It is no more his than it is the bank president's. Therefore, would he not be foolish to pretend that, because he was driving a truck full of gold, he was better than the man driving the garbage truck for the city? Very likely the garbage-truck driver gets a much bigger paycheck at the end of the week than the bank-truck driver, even though he has been carrying around with him throughout the week a much less enviable load.

It will be the same in Heaven. Persons with few gifts, with meager talent, or looks, or abilities, or achievement may get the much greater reward, because of the humble way they did their work for God with what they had, than the persons with all the talents, and all looks, and all the ability, but who attributed their gifts to themselves so foolishly and sought and basked in their own glory.

Therefore, humility does not at all mean denying the gifts, and the abilities, and the talent, and attributes that Almighty God has given us; it does mean that we attribute them not to ourselves but to God. It demands that we use them, not for our own display, not for getting the praise of others, but to be useful to ourselves and others and thereby give glory to God. If we are humble, we use our gifts of nature and grace to do good; we use them to spread God's kingdom and His glory. We follow the counsel of our divine Lord: "Let your light shine before men, in order that they may see your good works and give glory to your Father in Heaven."[72] Let your light shine before

---

[72] Matt. 5:16.

men, He tells us. That is, do not hide your light under a bushel; do not conceal the talents and abilities that you have. Use them, but use them for the glory of God.

If, as a result of our doing this, others praise us, let us refer the praise to God instead of proudly soaking it up ourselves. We can say in reply to a compliment, "Well, God is good." Or, if we are tempted to feel proud over anything God has given us or done through us, we should strive to develop the habit of praying silently, "Not to us, O Lord, not to us, but to Thy name give glory," as the psalmist said.[73] To attribute what we have to God, where the credit belongs; to say, "God is good," when we are praised; to use our talents and abilities not for our own glory but for the glory of God: this is the positive practice of humility.

Humility can be manifested in
failures and in our conversation

Humility can be manifested, and in fact must be manifested, even in failure. Very often we are asked to do something for which we feel we do not have the ability, or the time, or the acumen to do a first-rate job. So, we try to get out of it. But that is not humility. If we are asked to do something by legitimate superiors, it is God asking us to do it. If we feel incompetent, we are permitted to state our reasons. But if, in spite of that, we are still asked to do it, we should do the best we can with what we have in the way of talent, ability, or material. If

---

[73] Ps. 113b:1 (RSV = Ps. 115:1).

we have done our best, God looks for nothing else and He is glorified by our effort and intention alone.

God does not judge us by the results we produce but by our efforts and intention. Even if our project does not turn out well, even if it is an outright failure, that failure is God's will, and it is a lot better for us than success in that instance. If we fail at any time, God keeps us humble thereby, and that is what counts in the ultimate analysis. If we succeed, we might give way to pride, and that would be worse than any material failure could possibly be. Humility, then, has a great place in our attitude toward and ability to cope with failure, which we all inevitably face at one time or another.

It is also manifested in our conversation by letting others choose the subject, and by speaking little of ourselves. We must not be one of those who have a very clever and ingenious way of swinging every topic and every subject around to some situation or some slant in which they can take the conversational ball and carry it for a long period. They maneuver the trend of conversation so that they can dominate the group with the story of their exploits, of what they have done, of what they can do. This, in spite of the fact that if they had studied the slightest bit of anatomy, they could tell by the way their arms are hung that they were not made to pat themselves on the back. "What hast thou that thou hast not received? And if thou hast received it, why dost thou boast as if thou hadst not received it?" What have we done that God has not given us the wherewithal to do? And if we have received the wherewithal to do what we do, why do we glory as if we have not received it?

❧

Humility will help you bear
unsought humiliations

Again, the practice of humility is demanded, perhaps most frequently, in the acceptance of little humiliations which come to us unlooked for, the kind of humiliations we do not seek, but which Almighty God sends us directly. They are the best sort of humiliations for which to be alert.

When others express contempt for us, when our talents are overlooked, when we receive bad treatment, when others are chosen to do something that we would like to do — or something that we feel we could do better than the ones chosen — or when we receive corrections and advice: these are all God-given opportunities to practice humility by accepting them graciously.

On the other hand, to accuse and excuse is a mark of pride; to accuse others for mistakes we make and excuse ourselves is the mark of a proud person. How easy it is to say in self-defense: "The reason that turned out that way was because So-and-so said such-and-such"; or, "I was going to do it that way but So-and-so said not to." We blame everybody else, accuse everybody for our failures and faults, and excuse ourselves. Doing so proclaims our pride!

But the humble are ever ready to accuse themselves. Recall the Pharisee and the publican. Hear the Pharisee accusing the poor publican: "I thank You, God, that I am not like the rest of men . . . or even like this publican." But the poor publican did not accuse anybody but himself. He didn't even think to excuse himself: "O God, be merciful to me, a sinner." But our

Lord said that the publican went down to his house justified rather than the other.[74]

Strive to put up with humiliations

There are several attitudes we can take toward humiliations that come to us unsought: we can rebel against them; we can merely accept them; or we can accept them cheerfully or even look for them. If we rebel against them, it is bad, because then we are rebelling against the will of God; we are rebelling against what God is sending us and what God wills to happen to us. Thus, we must struggle not to rebel against humiliations.

We must at least accept them — that is, put up with them, take them without rebellion. If we do, it is good. We then have at least a manifestation of the virtue of humility — namely, to accept humiliations without resentment and without rebellion.

Those who are better, the more advanced in the spiritual life, not only accept humiliations, but accept them cheerfully, because they thereby imitate our divine Lord more closely. They are more like our Lord on the Cross. They accept humiliations cheerfully, because thus they can participate more fully in His apostolate of salvation for the world; thus they can share more actively in His redemptive work.

The good, then, put up with or accept humiliation; the better, the more advanced, are cheerful in the face of humiliations. Finally, the best, the saints, go looking for humiliations. They seek out contradictions because they love the Cross of

[74] Cf. Luke 18:10-14.

Christ so much they want to seek it, rather than wait for it to come, so that more and more they may be co-redeemers with Christ.

But, at the very least, we must strive to be good, that is, to accept and put up with the humiliations we meet day by day. If, in our pride, we rebel against them, we are telling God that we don't deserve what He is sending us. But that is not the truth, and therefore, we are not humble.

Admittedly, it is a long, hard road to acquire facility in the virtue of humility. But it is a goal that will never be reached unless we start. Furthermore, there is no time like the present to begin to acquire this facility. If we ever think that we have reached it, and that we can rest on our oars, just recall this fact: if we can be humiliated, we still are not humble.

Chapter 11

✼

Persevere

Finally we come to an end of our discussion of some basic spiritual means for living a healthy spiritual life. But do not be in the least discouraged at what may seem a discouraging task in life. Our goal has been presented clearly, but we are not at the goal; perhaps we are not expected to be at the goal. But if the goal were never pointed out to us, we would never begin to strive for it. For that reason, the objective has been delineated, and motives and means have been urged for striving toward it.

But, be it repeated, let no one be discouraged in that striving, for if we are discouraged, it is because we are trusting in ourselves and not in God. As a warning to those who trust in themselves, our Lord has said, "Without me you can do nothing."[75] But to those who trust in Him, He has given the words of St. Paul: "I can do all things in Him who strengthens me."[76]

Our determination, our conviction, then, should be to trust in God; to recognize that all He wants is our puny efforts; that all He wants is for us to say, "Dear God, I will *try*, but I know You will be behind me, doing the work. I won't be the

[75] John 15:5.
[76] Phil. 4:13.

one who is doing it." What He wants is for us to try, just to try. Above all, He wants us to tell Him with all our hearts we at least *want* to try. He wants us even to pray to be able to say, "Dear God, I want to try." He will be satisfied with that for a beginning. And if we pray to Mary, she cannot help obtaining that grace for us, the grace to say to her Son with all our heart, "Dear God, you know I want to try."

Philip E. Dion

(1910-1994)

⚹

Not every priest has a nun for a mother. But Fr. Philip Dion was able to claim that distinction when, in 1948, his widowed mother received from his hands the habit of the Sisters of the Good Shepherd in Halifax, Nova Scotia, and became Sr. Mary of St. Vincent de Paul.

Born in Boston, Philip Dion attended St. Joseph's Seminary, in Princeton, New Jersey, in 1928, but after two years, tuberculosis compelled him to leave the seminary for eight years. Those years of mandatory rest allowed him to read extensively and to develop skills that would serve him well in his later seminary studies and in his ministry. He was ordained a Vincentian priest in 1941.

Fr. Dion was a gifted teacher, beginning at Niagara University and later teaching at St. John's University in New York City, where he served as Academic Dean from 1952-1954. In 1954, he became the assistant director of the Daughters of Charity in Emmitsburg, Maryland. There he taught the nuns in their mother house and taught at St. Joseph's College, of which he was Chairman of the Board. After spending a year studying in Rome, Fr. Dion was assigned to the Seminary of Our Lady of the Angels, in Albany, New York, in 1961, where he taught, preached retreats, and served as spiritual director and Academic Dean.

In 1976, Fr. Dion assumed administrative duties in the office of the Central Association of the Miraculous Medal, in Philadelphia, where he edited the association's magazine and promoted devotion to the Blessed Virgin Mary at the Shrine of the Miraculous Medal, in Germantown, Pennsylvania. Three years later he was named the Provincial Director of Aging and Retirement, and in 1985, he became the Director of the Vincentian Missions and raised funds to support Vincentian missionaries overseas.

Fr. Dion wrote five books and numerous articles that reflect his ease with using stories, jokes, and anecdotes to illustrate and reinforce his points — a skill that made him a popular and effective teacher and writer. Written with humor, compassion, and encouragement, and distilling profound theological truths so that even non-theologians can understand them with perfect clarity, Fr. Dion's works offer today's readers both the motivation and the means to grow in spiritual perfection.

Sophia Institute

Sophia Institute is a nonprofit institution that seeks to nurture the spiritual, moral, and cultural life of souls and to spread the Gospel of Christ in conformity with the authentic teachings of the Roman Catholic Church.

Sophia Institute Press fulfills this mission by offering translations, reprints, and new publications that afford readers a rich source of the enduring wisdom of mankind.

Sophia Institute also operates two popular online Catholic resources: CrisisMagazine.com and CatholicExchange.com.

Crisis Magazine provides insightful cultural analysis that arms readers with the arguments necessary for navigating the ideological and theological minefields of the day. *Catholic Exchange* provides world news from a Catholic perspective as well as daily devotionals and articles that will help you to grow in holiness and live a life consistent with the teachings of the Church.

In 2013, Sophia Institute launched Sophia Institute for Teachers to renew and rebuild Catholic culture through service to Catholic education. With the goal of nurturing the spiritual, moral, and cultural life of souls, and an abiding respect for the role and work of teachers, we strive to provide materials and programs that are at once enlightening to the mind and ennobling to the heart; faithful and complete, as well as useful and practical.

Sophia Institute gratefully recognizes the Solidarity Association for preserving and encouraging the growth of our apostolate over the course of many years. Without their generous and timely support, this book would not be in your hands.

www.SophiaInstitute.com
www.CatholicExchange.com
www.CrisisMagazine.com
www.SophiaInstituteforTeachers.org